THE INSTANT BOX GARDEN

MIRACLE

HOW TO GROW FOOD, FLOWERS AND HERBS IN SMALL SPACES

SUSAN PATTERSON, MASTER GARDENER

ALTERNATIVE
DAILY

CONTENTS

INTRODUCTION

Themes just seem to make everything more fun, even gardening. The idea of thematic gardens is not knew. Medicinal gardens, cut gardens, cottage gardens, butterfly gardens and more have been incorporated into landscapes throughout time and across cultures.

I started theme box gardens with my kids when they were young and it was a great way to encourage their interest in growing food and flowers. The whole family can get involved in planning, planting, and harvesting. Not only that, but it is also really satisfying to create tasty drinks, and dishes along with beautiful bouquets, creams, elixirs and crafts using the plants from your box garden.

Instant box gardens allow both novice and experienced gardeners the opportunity to enjoy thematic gardening on a manageable scale. This book contains two types of box gardens:

- The popular 4'x4' box garden is perfect for those who have a little garden space and don't mind bending down to plant, tend and harvest their gardens. Veggies and fruits requiring deeper soil levels are perfect for this type of bed.

- Elevated box gardens are a fantastic spin on the traditional box that allows anyone to grow a theme garden with only minimal space. These gardens are perfect for patios, balconies or any other small space. They are easy to plant and care for while offering endless rewards.

Come along with me as I share some of my favorite instant box garden themes. I know that you will be amazed at just how much food you can grow and how much beauty you can create in a very little space, not to mention all the fun you will have gardening.

Note: In this book you will find everything that you need to make creative, beautiful and delicious box gardens. Take a quick look at the Planting and Harvesting Guide section located at the back of this book. Use it as your handy reference for every plant you will find included in each garden since it includes planting and harvesting tips, along with other useful suggestions for success.

May all of your instant box gardens grow well,

Susan Patterson, *Master Gardener*

> Special Thanks to my husband Thomas who is always coming up with amazing ideas for the garden!

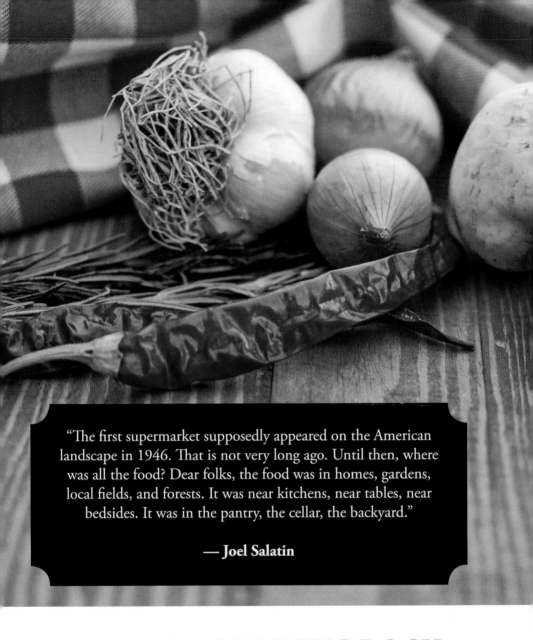

"The first supermarket supposedly appeared on the American landscape in 1946. That is not very long ago. Until then, where was all the food? Dear folks, the food was in homes, gardens, local fields, and forests. It was near kitchens, near tables, near bedsides. It was in the pantry, the cellar, the backyard."

— **Joel Salatin**

WHY BOX GARDENS ROCK

You might be wondering why box gardens are so popular. There are a number of advantages to containing a garden in a box versus growing one in the ground, including:

Convenience

Box gardening can be done in a very small space, making it a convenient way for anyone to grow food. Even if you live in an apartment or have a tiny patio or a small yard, you can have a robust garden. If you have always been too busy in the past to tend a garden, a box style is a great choice for you because it is easy to manage. There are fewer weeds, and those that do appear are much easier to pull out because the soil is not packed hard by foot traffic.

Economics

When you grow a conventional row garden, there tends to be quite a bit of waste. With box gardening, nothing goes to waste, and each box of robust crops provides more than enough food to feed a small family. You won't miss the expenses and pollutants associated with conventional gardens such as irrigation, fertilizers, and pesticides. With this zero waste garden model, you will use all you grow!

Accessibility

One of the great things about box gardening is that anyone can do it. This form of gardening makes it easy for the young or old to grow a bountiful harvest. Gardens can be adapted and raised so that those with back or knee problems or in a wheelchair can also enjoy gardening.

Portability

The simple design of box gardens makes it easy to pick up and move. If you are interested in moving a conventional garden, it takes quite a bit of effort to find a new location and create a suitable growing space.

Health

Not only is growing your own produce great for your physical health but there is solid research supporting the fact that tending a garden has a host of therapeutic benefits that are enhanced by the fact that planting a box garden is so easy. Spending just a little time each day taking care of your garden is relaxing and can reduce stress after a hard day's work.

Extended Growing Season

Boxed gardens are raised slightly above the ground, in some cases quite a bit above the ground. This creates favorable growing conditions for plants which allows you to enjoy a fresh harvest long after conventional gardens have petered out for the season.

Better Soil

Conventional gardening soil often requires a great deal of amending and monitoring to get it just right. One of the best things about square box gardening is that you can control the quality of the planting medium from the very beginning; and keeping it healthy is pretty easy. Creating your own "best" soil mixture will give your plants everything they need to be healthy and productive.

Fewer Weeds, Pests and Diseases

Box gardens (especially elevated gardens) are safe from weeds, ground-dwelling pests and soil-borne fungal diseases. This makes maintenance even easier. NO need for back-breaking weed pulling or dangerous pesticides or herbicides.

Environmentally Friendly

Growing your own food is environmentally friendly. A tremendous amount of fuel is used to harvest, store, and transport produce to your local grocery store, not to mention all the waste used for packaging. Not only does growing your own food provide you and your family with fresh ingredients, it also reduces your carbon footprint. Now that's something you can feel good about.

PLANTING AND CARE

Starting Seeds

Starting seeds is an economical and fun way to grow plants for your box gardens. Although growing seeds is not difficult, here are a few best practice tips that will help you have the most success.

- Start with fresh, high-quality seed-starting mix. Don't use standard potting mix, which isn't fine or light enough for germinating seeds. Consider using coconut coir which is a renewable resource made from coconut fibers. It retains moisture and nutrients well.

- Read the seed packet carefully before you begin. Some seeds, especially tiny ones, can be just pressed into the surface of the moist seed starting mix. Others, like cucumbers, are covered with more potting mix.

- If you're in doubt, plant seeds about two or three times as deep as their width. Keep in mind that planting seeds too shallow is always better than too deep because too much potting mix will block the light.

- Don't start your seeds too early. Read the container for specific information, but in general, most seeds should be planted four to six weeks before you can safely transplant them outdoors after the last frost of the season.

- Be ready for some losses and don't be discouraged; it's normal for a certain number of seeds not to germinate.

- Use clean containers. The type of container doesn't matter as long as it has a drainage hole in the bottom. Some people prefer coconut coir pots or seedling flats, but you can also use cottage cheese containers or plastic beverage cups.

- Invest in a heat mat, which will provide gentle heat that keeps the potting mix consistently warm until the seeds germinate. If you're only planting a few seeds, put the containers on top of a refrigerator or other warm appliance. (No lights are needed for germination).

- Be sure to label the containers so you don't forget what you planted. Mark the containers with a permanent marker, or write the name of the plant on popsicle sticks.

- Cover the containers with clear plastic to keep the atmosphere warm and moist.

- Remove the plastic and place the containers under lights when the seedlings are about half an inch tall. Without adequate light, seedlings will be tall, spindly, and more prone to disease. You may be tempted to place the seedlings near a window, but light from a window is inconsistent and rarely bright enough.

- Although you can purchase grow lights, plants do just as well under less expensive fluorescent shop lights. Put one warm bulb and one cool bulb in each fixture.

- Leave the lights on for 12 to 14 hours every day. A timer is a good investment if you tend to be forgetful.

- Be sure to water seedlings consistently. A spray bottle with a mister works fine if you're starting only a few seeds, but a turkey baster works better for large numbers of containers.

- Be careful not to overwater; excessively soggy soil is the number one reason for seed-starting failure. The seed starting mix should be moist, but not dripping wet.

- Brush the palm of your hand gently over the tops of the seedlings to promote stronger stems. A fan set on low and placed near the seedlings serves the same purpose.

- Once true leaves appear (following the tiny seedling leaves), begin feeding the seedlings every week. Use a general-purpose, water-soluble fertilizer mixed to half strength.

- Keep the seedlings indoors until you're absolutely sure the last frost of the season has passed. A sudden cold snap can make short work of your carefully tended plants.

- At this point, it's essential to "harden off" the seedlings, which gives them time to acclimate to the cooler outdoor air. Begin by placing them in a sunny, protected outdoor spot for about an hour every day for three days, preferably in the morning. Increase their time outdoors for an hour or two every day for a week. By that time, the seedlings should be strong enough for transplanting.

Soil

One of the key factors to the success of your box garden is the planting medium that you use. The biggest mistake that you can make when filling your box garden is to use only potting soil or compost. If you do this, your soil will drain too quickly and will wash away essential nutrients. Reserve organic material like straw, grass or wood chips for topping your beds to help with moisture retention. Never work these elements into your soil - top dress only for best results. Never add fresh organic material like chicken, sheep, goat, horse or cow manure into your box garden. It is critical that it be composted first.

Here is the best planting mixture for your box garden:

- **1 part - Vermiculite** - Vermiculite looks like a silver fleck and is a mica-type material that is heated up and expanded to increase its ability to hold water. The particles soak up water and nutrients and hang on to them until plants are ready to use them. Be sure you purchase vermiculite from a garden shop.

- **1 part - Perlite** - Perlite looks like little pieces of styrofoam and is actually a volcanic mineral. It helps with drainage along with air and water retention.

- **2 parts - Aged animal compost** - Whether you purchase composted animal manure or make your own, be sure that it is well aged.

- **2 parts - Coconut coir** - Coconut coir is made from the husk of coconuts and is a totally renewable resource and completely sustainable - unlike peat moss or sphagnum moss that takes a hundred years to redevelop. Coconut coir keeps the soil aerated and retains both moisture and nutrients. It addition, it also has a neutral pH while peat or sphagnum is more acidic. It is light, easy to work with and perfect for elevated box gardens.

Transplants

For the healthiest plant, follow these easy steps when transplanting:

- Mark the grid for planting.

- Create a hole large enough for your transplants - sometimes a pencil works to make the hole. For larger plants, use a hand trowel.

- Remove transplant from the container being careful not to damage the roots.

- Place the transplant into the hole and gently pat down the soil to hold it in place.

- Create a small dip around the base of the plant that will hold water.

- Water the transplants gently and keep moist for several days until established.

- If you live in a very hot climate - provide a shade cloth for hot afternoon sun until transplants are established.

Food

All plants benefit from regular feeding, especially those in raised box gardens or containers. Here are some great goodies to add to your garden boxes.

- **Worm castings** - If you don't have your own worm farm, no worries, you can purchase worm poop by the bag. Use 1/4 bag for the 1' x 6' foot bed, ⅓ bag for the 1' x 4' bed and the 1' x 2' bed. Worm poop will enrich your planting medium greatly and provides much needed nitrogen for plants. Replenish your garden box with castings once a month during the growing season.

- **Azomite** - Azomite rock dust has a ton of minerals and trace elements that are great for your gardens. Add 1/2 lb for each 1' x 6' bed and 1/4 lb for the 1' x 4' bed and the 1' x 2' bed.

- **Fish emulsion water** - Fish emulsion is made from whole fish or parts of fish and is an overall nutrient booster that provides plants with nitrogen, phosphorus, potassium and trace elements.

- **Compost tea** - Compost tea is a great way to naturally strengthen and feed plants. It is a very rich and well balanced organic supplement that is made by steeping aged compost in water. While you can make it at home, you can also purchase this pre-made. Follow package directions for regular feeding.

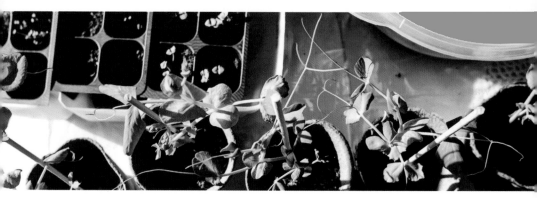

Weeds and Pests

Because box gardens are planted so densely, it not only makes it difficult to weed the beds but also, and thankfully, reduces the need to do so. The sides of boxed gardens create somewhat of a block for blowing seeds as well as most rhizomous plants. If you use a clean potting mixture, you should find that you have few, if any, weeds to worry about.

Keeping your plants healthy through proper feeding and watering will also discourage any widespread attack by pests. A light sprinkle of diatomaceous earth on and around your plants will also set up a great defense against any pests that do happen to land in your garden.

Water

Like container gardens, box gardens (especially elevated box gardens) require more water than conventional gardens. It is crucial that your box gardens have ample drainage and that you pay particular attention to watering. Water plants thoroughly when soil is dry. Good watering practices make a huge difference. This includes watering only in the early morning or evenings and only when plants need it. Seedlings require more water than mature plants but mature plants need deep watering to develop solid roots. Water at least six to ten inches down. Be sure to test your box garden in several places after you water.

Placement

It is a good idea to think about placement before you plant your box garden. Although smaller gardens will not be difficult to move, it is still a good idea to plan ahead. Most fruits and vegetables need six to eight hours of full sun. If you are growing flowers that need sun, the rule is generally the same. Leafy greens and a number of herbs prefer dappled hot afternoon sun. Be sure to review the light requirements of all plants before placing your bed.

Avoid placing a 4'x4' box garden box where it will be easily saturated with water. Not only will too much water compromise the structural components of your bed, but it will also spoil your gardening fun and plant quality. If you have no choice, add some sand to raise up the area where you wish to place your garden box. You can also build it off the ground by adding a bottom and some blocks or legs.

Replanting

In all but the coldest climates, you will be able to get two to three crops per year out of each grow box in your garden. Consider the two types of crops - cool-weather crops do best in early spring and the fall but not great in the heat of the summer. Warm, or hot weather crops need the heat to survive and don't do as well in the early spring and fall. One of the best things about box gardening is that you can grow a full crop of cool-season vegetables then a warm season crop and follow that up with a cool season fall crop. Do your homework when planning out your garden to maximize the space you have for an ultimate harvest.

Cover Crops

Don't let your box garden sit empty all winter but plant a cover crop at the end of the season, such as barley, oats or winter rye. This will put nutrients back into your soil.

THE ANATOMY OF
A 4'X4' BOX GARDEN

Growing plants in a simple raised bed is also known as intensive or friendship gardening. This style of growing is based on the idea that there are a number of plants that actually like to grow close together and do better when planted this way, a simple box garden is a raised bed with 16 x 1' growing boxes that offer the ability for crops to be planted in succession throughout the growing season. This type of gardening makes growing food for yourself and an entire family easy.

Special Tips for 4'x4' Box Garden Success

- When planting your box be sure to keep tall plants on the north side of the garden. This keeps them from shading other plants. Plant lettuce and other plants that like a little shade on the east side of the box to keep them directly out of afternoon sun.

- Be thinking about vertical space. Arbors, walls, fences and trellis structures will help increase your yield without taking up more space. Plants such as peas, pole beans, squashes and cucumbers love to grow upwards.

- Position low growing plants in the outside planting squares.

- Always make a drawing of your planting design and keep if for future reference.

Building a 4'x4' Box Garden

If you have the space and want to create a larger garden, this 4'x4' box is easy to build. This size of bed offers up 16 twelve inch planting squares which is a great amount of growing space. You don't need any special tools or building skills to construct this simple box and planting grid.

| What you need |

Box

2 pieces of 2"x6"x8' pine or
   redwood, cut in half

4ft wide landscape fabric or thick
   layers of cardboard

6" wood screws

Drill

1/8" drill bit

Water sealant

Grid

6 pieces, 1"x1"x4'1" of ½"
   pre-cut wood (very thin, used to
   delineate boxes)

Tape measure

Attach Screw

Box

1   Lay the four pieces of wood on their sides and connect using the wood screws - to form a box.

2   Coat the box with a protective sealant - especially if you use pine.

3   Place the completed frame in a level area chosen for your garden.

4   Lay down landscape fabric, cardboard (or both).

5   Add soil mixture and grid.

Grid

1   Measure and place your grid pieces evenly across the soil to create 16 12" inch growing boxes.

4ft

Square Box

2x6

12"

12"

4ft

12"

pre cut
1"x 1/2" x 4'1/2"
long

12"

12"   12"   12"   12"

4'X4' BOX GARDEN THEMES

Always choose plants that are best suited for your growing area. If you are unsure, visit a local nursery for help. Many plants can be started from seed. Where varieties of plants are not suggested, feel free to choose as desired.

Easy Peasy Variety Food Box Garden

If you are new to gardening, this theme will produce plenty of produce, herbs and beautiful flowers and give you a chance to grow your "green thumb." The combination of food, flowers and herbs makes this an all around spectacular visual display producing a significant harvest.

Box Type: 4'x4'

Planting Boxes: 16

Plants:

- Jack Be Little Pumpkin
- Echinacea
- Sugar Baby Watermelon
- Dwarf Sunflower
- Broccoli
- Roma Tomato
- Marigold
- Basil

- Lettuce
- Spinach
- Beets
- Bush beans
- Onions
- Carrots
- Radish

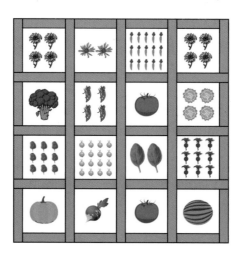

Try This: Keep a Harvest Calendar

With such an exciting variety of plants in a single bed, it can be a little confusing to keep track of planting and harvest times for all of your produce. Hang a large paper calendar in your garden shed (or mudroom), or use the calendar app on your phone or computer to organize your plants. Write down when you need to purchase seeds, when you need to start each particular plant, and when you should transplant to the garden. Estimate when your vegetables will be ready for harvest and indicate that on your calendar as well so that no ripe veggie gets left behind.

You Can "Can It" Garden

This box garden is loaded with fresh produce that lends itself well to canning. There is nothing quite so rewarding as enjoying your garden harvest all year. Canning is one timeless way to preserve fruits and veggies so you can experience their fresh taste even in the dead of winter.

Box Type: 4'x4'

Planting Boxes: 16

Plants:

- Nantes Scarlet Half Long Carrots
- Southport White Globe Onion
- Brandywine Tomato
- Long Green Cucumber

- Bush Bean
- Bullose Sweet Pepper
- Dukat Dill
- Detroit Dark Red Beats

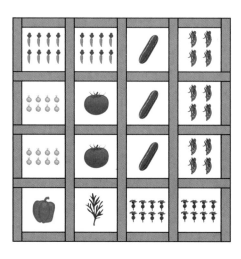

Try This: Canning 101

Canning isn't just for your grandmother. Follow these simple steps to preserve your produce and embrace a more sustainable lifestyle. This waterbath method is incredibly easy and you don't need any special equipment. Let's get started!

1   Place your canning pot on the stove filled about halfway with water. Cover and bring to a boil and then reduce to a simmer. This process will take a while so it is good to get started on it early.

2   Use only the best produce. No slightly mushy beets or spotty tomatoes should make the cut. Use your best judgement and select veggies that are worth canning. Enjoy the rest fresh.

3   Wash the jars. Even if they seem clean, wash them again with warm soapy water or run them through the dishwasher. Rinse the lids and bands by hand.

4   Sterilize the jars by submerging them in your canning pot for at least 15 minutes. Place lids in a large bowl and pour boiling water over them.

5   Follow your desired canning recipe and fill your jars, leaving headspace as recommended by the recipe between the lid and the vegetables. Screw the lid on tightly.

6   It will be helpful to have a jar lifter to submerge the jars in water and avoid burning your fingers.

7   Place jar in canner, ensuring that it is covered by at least 2 inches of water. Place lid on canner and bring to a rolling boil. Boil for amount of time indicated in the recipe and then turn off heat and remove lid.

8   Allow jars to rest in the canner for at least five minutes and then leave at room temperature for 12-24 hours. Do not disturb jars or try to adjust lids.

9   Inspect the lid for seals. There should be no flex when the center is pressed in.

10   Store for up to 18 months in a cool, dark place.

THE ANATOMY OF AN ELEVATED BOX GARDEN

The idea behind a box garden with legs is to make planting and care easy as well as to allow those with limited space to enjoy growing beautiful plants without the need for an expansive garden space.

Elevated box gardens are a hybrid gardening technique that is basically half container gardening and half raised bed gardening. Traditional raised garden beds sit directly on the ground and often don't have a bottom. Containers do have a bottom to contain soil but are generally smaller than raised beds. Elevated box gardens provide the best of both worlds. They have a bottom and can be big enough in size (depending on space and needs) to grow a bountiful harvest or beautiful display of flowers and herbs. Not only that, but you can combine boxes to make a substantial garden in a relatively small space.

The key to a successful box garden has to do with choice of plants, spacing and location of the box. The easiest way to plan, plant and care for a box garden is to divide the growing space into 1 foot planting squares and make sure that you place your box where you can easily maintain it and it receives enough sunlight to thrive. Once you have these things down, the sky's the limit when it comes to designing and enjoying your very own box gardens.

Building Plans for Elevated Box Gardens

The theme beds that follow use three elevated bed sizes including:

1'x6' - 6 planting boxes

1'x4' - 4 planting boxes

1'x2' - 2 planting boxes

Each thematic garden plan that follows uses two box gardens of the same size. You can position the beds next to each other to form a larger bed or place them in different areas on your patio, balcony or deck. You can also choose to plant just one of the box gardens depending on your needs and desires or even mix and match box garden sizes. I have just given you suggestions and ideas to get you started.

These box gardens are easy enough to make at home, flexible enough to be used in a small space and sturdy enough to withstand the weight of the soil and plants. All of the designs below call for precut wood pieces which makes assembly a snap! You can also swap out pine for cedar (which will cost more) but is more durable. If your beds will be exposed to the weather, consider finishing them with an all weather protectant, just make sure it is not toxic if you are using the box for growing something to eat.

Tools Used for All Beds Include

Drill

⅛" drill bit

½" drill bit

Measuring tape

Pencil

Waterproof sealant

Brush

Fabric liner (optional)

Building a 1'x2' Elevated Box Garden

Supplies:

3 pieces of 1"x12" (wide)
   cut at 2' (long sides and
   bottom piece)

2 pieces of 1"x12"
   cut at 12.5" (end pieces)

4 pieces of 1"x4"
   cut at 30" (legs)

2 pieces of 1"x4"
   cut at 14" (braces)

Deck screws

| To Make: |

1. Lay the bottom piece on a flat surface.

2. Measure every three inches starting from end on side pieces and mark.

3. Predrill holes using ⅛" bit.

4. Attach side pieces to the bottom on the outside using deck screws.

5. Measure and mark the end pieces every three inches starting from the end.

6. Predrill holes using ⅛" bit.

7. Attach end pieces to the sides and bottom using deck screws.

8. You now have created the box.

9. Turn the box on its side and attach the leg pieces to the corners of the box using six deck screws for each leg.

10. Measure nine inches from the bottom of the box and mark as a guide for where the braces will go.

11. Attach brace pieces (on each side) using four deck screws.

12. Drill staggered drainage holes using a ½" drill bit.

13. Coat the inside of the box with food grade waterproof sealant and let dry.

14. Cut and place a fabric liner for the bottom (optional).

Building a 1'x4' Elevated Box Garden

3 pieces of 1"x12"
cut at 4" (sides and bottom piece)

2 pieces of 1"x12"
cut at 12.5" (end pieces)

4 pieces of 1"x4"
cut at 30" (legs)

2 pieces of 1"x4"
cut at 14" (brace pieces)

Deck Screws

To Make:

1. Lay the bottom piece on a flat surface.

2. Measure every four inches starting from end on side pieces and mark.

3. Predrill holes using ⅛" bit.

4. Attach side pieces to the bottom on the outside using deck screws.

5. Measure on the end pieces every four inches starting from the end and mark.

6. Predrill holes using ⅛" bit.

7. Attach end pieces to the sides and bottom using deck screws.

8. You now have created the box.

9. Turn the box on its side and attach the leg pieces to the corners of the box using six deck screws for each leg.

10. Measure nine inches from the bottom of the box and mark as a guide for where the braces will go.

11. Attach brace pieces (on each side) using four deck screws.

12. Drill staggered drainage holes using a ½" drill bit .

13. Coat the inside of the box with food grade waterproof sealant and let dry.

14. Cut and place a fabric liner for the bottom (optional).

Building a 1'x6' Elevated Box Garden

Supplies:

3 pieces of 1"x12" cut at 6' (sides and bottom piece)

2 pieces of 1"x12" cut at 12.5" (end pieces)

4 pieces of 1"x4" cut at 30 "(leg pieces)

2 pieces of 1"x4" cut at 14" (brace pieces)

Deck screws

1   Lay the bottom piece on a flat surface.

2   Measure every three inches starting from end on side pieces and mark.

3   Predrill holes using ⅛" bit.

4   Attach side pieces to the bottom on the outside using deck screws.

5   Measure on the end pieces every three inches starting from the end and mark.

6   Predrill holes using ⅛" bit.

7   Attach end pieces to the sides and bottom using deck screws.

8   You now have created the box.

9   Turn the box on its side and attach the leg pieces to the corners of the box using six deck screws for each leg.

10 Measure nine inches from the bottom of the box and mark as a guide for where the braces will go.

11 Attach brace pieces (on each side) using four deck screws.

12 Drill staggered drainage holes using a ½" drill bit.

13 Coat the inside of the box with food grade waterproof sealant and let dry.

14 Cut and place a fabric liner for the bottom (optional).

ATTACHING BRACE

Optional

To make planting boxes within each bed use ½ " x 1" x 12 ½ " pieces of pine. There will be 2 planting boxes in the 1'x2' bed, 4 planting boxes in the 1'x4' bed and 6 planting boxes in the 1'x6' bed. Attach these dividers using deck screws. Just make sure it is not toxic if you are using the box to **grow food**.

ADDING OPTIONAL GRID

ELEVATED BOX GARDEN THEMES

Always choose plants that are best suited for your growing area. If you are unsure, visit a local nursery for help. Many plants can be started from seed if desired. However, you can also follow the garden layouts for the number of mature plants per planting box. Where varieties of plants are not suggested, feel free to choose as desired.

Remember: Each theme uses two boxes, however, pick and choose what works best for you. If you have enough room, plant both boxes or just one if space is an issue. You can also adjust any of the themes to fit a 4'x4' planting box.

Get as creative as you want here! You can use mature plants, transplants or plant by seed. The number of plants depicted in each growing box represents mature plants, not seeds.

Sweet and Spicy Salsa Garden

There's nothing like fresh, sun-ripened tomatoes, flavorful cilantro, and spicy peppers to create that perfect homegrown garden salsa. Make some to serve right away at picnics, or parties and freeze or preserve the rest for winter. Don't forget to share!

Box Type: 1' x 4' plus 1' x 4'

Planting Boxes: 8

Plants:

Roma Tomato

Red Beard Scallions

Leaf Cilantro

Bell Pepper/Jalapeno

Peppermint

Silverskin Garlic

Stevia

Box A

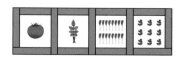

Box B

TRY THIS:

Sweet and Spicy Salsa

This delicious recipe is a perfect way to use all those fresh ingredients from your salsa bed.

Ingredients:

4 ripe tomatoes, cored and quartered

1 onion, peeled and quartered

3 garlic cloves, peeled

3 jalapenos (or bell pepper for a more mild salsa), stemmed and seeded

1/3 cup fresh cilantro

3 Tbsp fresh lime juice

1 Tbsp ground cumin

2 tsp powdered stevia

1 ½ tsp salt

2 cups finely diced tomatoes

¼ cup mint leaves, loosely packed

¼ cup chopped scallions for topping

Instructions:

1 Add all ingredients except tomatoes to blender or food processor. Pulse until all ingredients are well combined.

2 Add in tomatoes and pulse until desired consistency is reached.

3 Chill until ready to serve. Top with scallions.

4 Store in airtight container in the refrigerator for up to 1 week.

Petite Patio Salad Garden

Vibrant, vitamin rich greens along with crunchy cucumbers, juicy tomatoes, and crisp radishes with a bite make this raw veggie garden absolutely irresistible. Having a salad garden means that you know exactly where your fresh produce comes from and that it hasn't been subjected to any nasty chemicals or harmful manipulation. This sweet little bed is perfect for urban dwellers who want to grow their own salad. You can easily expand this plan for a larger area or more people.

Box Type: 1'x4' plus 1'x4'

Planting Boxes: 8

Plants:

 Cherry Tomato

 Mini Munch Cucumber

 Cherry Belle Radishes

 Arugula

 Green Leaf Lettuce

 Banana Peppers

Swiss Chard

Box A

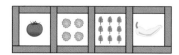

Box B

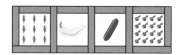

TRY THIS:

Fresh Spring Salad

Adjust salad ingredients to fit seasonal produce and enjoy as a side or main dish with grilled chicken.

Ingredients:

½ cup arugula, chopped

1 cup lettuce, chopped

½ cup Swiss chard

¼ cup banana pepper, chopped

¼ cup radish, chopped

1 cucumber, diced

1 tomato, diced

1/2 cup cashews

Dressing ingredients:

3 Tbsp olive oil

1 Tbsp freshly-squeezed lemon juice

1 tsp Dijon mustard

1 small clove garlic, finely-minced

1/2 tsp fine sea salt

1/4 tsp freshly-cracked black pepper

2 Tbsp raw honey

Instructions:

1 Add all salad ingredients to a large bowl.

2 Whisk salad dressing to combine and drizzle over salad.

3 Toss to combine. Serve immediately.

Cocktail Garden

Amp up your evening mixer by including any of these tasty ingredients in your favorite drinks. Your cocktail wizardry will go unrivaled with fragrant lavender, sweet basil, and indulgent strawberries. Grab the shaker bottle and get to work. Cheers!

Box Size: 1'x6' plus 1'x6'

Planting Boxes: 12

Plants

 Blue Boy Rosemary

 Dasher II Cucumber

 Italian Flat-Leaf Parsley

 Cherry Tomato

 Spearmint

 Lemon Verbena

 Sweet Basil

 Lavender

 Alpine Strawberry

 Leaf Cilantro

Box A

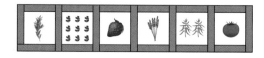

Box B

TRY THIS:

Cucumber Basil Twist

This refreshing garden cocktail is a perfect way to wind down after a busy week.

Ingredients:

Four 1/2-inch-thick slices of cucumber, plus thin cucumber slices for garnish

2 large basil leaves, plus small basil leaves for garnish

1 1/2 oz silver tequila, such as Patron

1/2 oz fresh lime juice

1/2 oz simple syrup

Ice

Instructions:

1 Combine thick cucumber slices and large basil leaves in cocktail shaker and muddle well with wooden spoon.

2 Add in remaining ingredients and shake well.

3 Serve over ice with basil and cucumber for garnish.

Lavender Vanilla Mixer

Oozing with the relaxing taste of lavender, this mixer will be a hit at your next gathering.

Ingredients:

Ice

1 ½ ounces vanilla vodka

½ oz fresh lemon juice

¼ oz Lavender Syrup

1 fresh lavender sprig

Instructions:

1 Fill cocktail shaker with ice and add all ingredients.

2 Shake well to combine.

3 Pour into chilled martini glass and garnish with fresh lavender.

A Fine Cup of Tea Garden

This fragrant garden is sure to peak the interest of any tea fanatic or herb lover. Strong and subtle flavors combine to form the ultimate herbal tea garden with stevia to bring a natural sweetness. Time for a tea party!

Box Type: 1'x4' plus 1'x4'

Planting Boxes: 8

Plants:

 English Lavender

 Lemon Balm

 Chocolate Mint

 German Chamomile

 Herb Fennel

 Stevia Rebaudiana

 Common Sage

 Sweet Marjoram

Box A

Box B

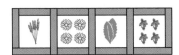

TRY THIS:

Soothing Herbal Tea

Collect a handful of fresh herbs or flowers listed above and add to boiling water. Steep for 5-7 minutes and strain through a fine sieve. You can also use a few teaspoons of dried herbs to make herbal tea by following the same instructions. Use the stevia from your garden to add a note of sweetness and enhance the flavor. Try combining different herbs to make your own tea blends. Suggested combinations include:

- Chamomile, mint, stevia
- Lavender, sage, stevia
- Lemon balm, marjoram, stevia

Collect and dry any extra herbs and place in small, airtight baggies. Give your friends and family your homegrown tea blends as gifts.

Seed Sharing Garden

Creating a gift that can grow is one of the best ways to show you care. Seeds are incredibly easy to collect and will help you create a beautiful, self-sustaining garden and robust seed collection in just a few years. Use your seed packets as homemade gifts to share the joy of new growth!

Bed Type: 1'x4' plus 1'x4'

Planting Boxes: 8

Plants:

 Marbles Mix 4 O'Clocks

 Pacino Sunflower

 Salmon Baby Nasturtiums

 Heavenly Blue Morning Glory

 Black Coco Beans

 Yolo Wonder Bell Peppers

Box A

Box B

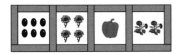

TRY THIS:

Seed Saving and Sharing

Create or connect with a gardeners club in your community. Encourage each other to save and trade seeds and you'll soon be growing new and exciting plants without having to spend a penny. Or, you can always donate extra seeds to a community garden that helps feed the hungry or contributes to a charitable organization. This is also a wonderful way to preserve heirloom varieties and continue passing them on to future generations.. Remember, hybrid varieties will not grow from seeds you collect so it is important that any plants you want to save seeds from are open-pollinated and heirloom.

Therapeutic Garden

Orange prescription bottles lined up in your medicine cabinet can be replaced with this living pharmacy right out your back door. Migraine-relieving feverfew, skin-soothing calendula, immune-boosting echinacea, and more! These beneficial herbs can help heal your body from the inside out.

Bed Type: 1'x4' plus 1'x4'

Planting Boxes: 8

Plants:

 Calendula (pot marigold)

 Echinacea (purple coneflower)

 White Wonder Feverfew

 Stinging Nettle

 French Dandelion

 St. John's Wort

Box A

Box B

TRY THIS:

Get Well Salad

Your medicinal herbs can be used for a number of purposes including, salves, tinctures, balms, poultices, lotions, teas, syrups, and infusions. Experiment by adjusting different recipes to suit what is in season in your garden and find out what works best for you.

Try whipping up this delicious salad to get all the wonderful medicinal benefits from dandelion. Fresh dandelion greens contain contain potent antioxidants, can help fight inflammation, may aid blood sugar control, reduce cholesterol, lower blood pressure, and help with weight loss.

Ingredients:

1 Tbsp finely chopped garlic

1 Tbsp fresh lemon juice

1/2 tsp coarse sea salt

½ tsp honey

1/4 cup olive oil

8 cups dandelion greens, large leaves torn in half

Instructions:

1　Combine lemon juice, honey, sugar, and garlic in a small bowl. Whisk until well blended.

2　Add greens to a salad bowl and drizzle dressing over dandelion leaves, tossing to combine.

3　Enjoy right away.

Always consult your doctor before starting or replacing any medication with herbal supplements.

Ultimate Pizza Garden

Who doesn't love pizza? Smooth, sweet, and savory combine in this pizza garden bursting with possibility and flavor. You can whip up a homemade pie quicker than delivery with these juicy tomatoes, fragrant herbs, and potent toppings.

Bed Type: 1'x6' plus 1'x6'

Planting Boxes: 12

Plants:

 Roma Tomato

 Sweet Basil

 Italian Parsley

 Greek Oregano

 Walla Walla Onions

 Bell Peppers

 Semi-Savory Spinach

Artichoke Garlic

Box A

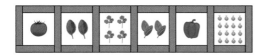

Box B

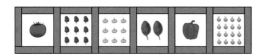

TRY THIS:

Fresh Homemade Pizza Sauce

Forget sauce in a jar. Try your hand at this delicious homemade sauce that will have your family asking for more.

Ingredients:

1 Tbsp. olive oil

1 Tbsp minced garlic

1 Tbsp fresh chopped oregano

1 Tbsp fresh chopped parsley

2 lbs diced fresh tomatoes

1 tsp honey

1/4 tsp pepper flakes

1/2 tsp kosher salt

Black pepper to taste

Instructions:

1   Warm olive oil over low heat in a medium sauce pot.

2   Add garlic and cook for about 1 minute or until it is fragrant.

3   Add tomatoes, red pepper, salt, pepper, and honey and turn heat to medium.

4   Bring to a boil, stirring frequently and reduce heat to low.

5   Simmer uncovered for 90 minutes, stirring occasionally.

6   Stir in parsley and oregano.

7   Blend with an immersion blender or puree in batches in a regular blender until smooth and no tomato chunks remain.

8   Spread desired amount over pizza crust and top with cheese, spinach, peppers, and caramelized onions. Enjoy!

Dried Goodness Garden

Every year, it seems like the vibrant burst of color at the peak of the growing season passes all too quickly. These easy-to-grow, everlasting annuals stay beautiful for months after they're dried and allow you to express your creativity with intriguing arrangements.

Bed Type: 1'x2' plus 1'x2'

Planting Boxes: 4

Plants:

 Statice

 Low Baby's Breath

 Sundaze Blaze Strawflower

 Dragon's Breath Celosia

Box A

Box B

TRY THIS:

Flower Drying 101

If you are just starting out with drying flowers, the process can seem a little intimidating. Thankfully, it is actually really simple and can be accomplished with just a few supplies. Follow these steps for exquisite dried flower bouquets that fill your home with lasting beauty.

1   Gather the flower stems in small bunches about ½" in diameter. Make sure to strip off lower leaves.

2   Tie stems together with a rubber band. Stems will shrink slightly so secure the band fairly tight.

3   Attach a string or hook and hang them upside down to best preserve the shape of the flowers.

4   Hang in a dry, dark area. The more sunlight the flowers are exposed to, the quicker the color will fade.

5   Leave ample space for air flow between bunches to reduce humidity and encourage drying.

Use floral foam in the bottom of a decorative vase to provide structure once you are ready to create your arrangement. Place taller stems with larger blooms in the center and fill in any empty spaces with baby's breath or dried greenery. You can also make your dried flowers into a wreath, potpourri, or bouquet. Experiment with different flower combinations and have fun!

Just "Kiddin" Around Garden

Soft and fuzzy lamb's ear, crunchy snap peas, and vibrant zinnias round out this versatile garden just for kids. Teach them the joy of planting with their very own box garden! Plus, these flowers and veggies are all quick to germinate and will provide plenty of excitement for kiddos with short attention spans.

Bed Type: 1'x4' plus 1'x4'

Planting Boxes: 8

Plants:

 Sugar Snap Peas

 Zinnias

 Little Finger Carrots

 Empress of India Nasturtiums

 Dwarf Sunflower

 Big Ears Lamb's Ear

Box A

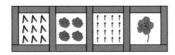

Box B

TRY THIS:

A Family Affair

Getting kids involved with gardening is an excellent way to teach them invaluable life lessons and instill in them a good work ethic, and an appreciation for the earth and healthy living. Here are a few tips to help you inspire your little ones to pick up a shovel and get their hands dirty.

1   **Get them their own tools.** Kids love small tools that are designed just for children with fun designs and patterns. This will help personalize the gardening experience and make it feel special.

2   **Let them plant the seeds.** Part of the fun of gardening is planting inconspicuous seeds and watching them grow into lively plants.

3   **Don't let the teaching stop in the garden.** When your child has a bundle of fresh carrots in hand, now is a great time to teach them how to wash and prepare their own fresh produce for a family meal.

4   **Flower and veggie stand.** Instead of a lemonade stand, encourage kids to set up a booth and sell their fresh cut flower arrangements or containers of crispy sweet snap peas. This will allow them to make a little money to buy their own seeds for the following year or finally get that toy they've had their eye on.

Sweet Succulent Garden

Succulents are all the rage these days for houseplant lovers. They are easy to care for, simple to grow and propagate, and can thrive even under the most forgetful waterer. But did you know that succulents have a place in your outdoor garden too? These fast-growing beauties will thrive for years to come!

Bed Type: 1'x2' plus 1'x2'

Planting Boxes: 4

Plants:

 Hens and Chicks (Common houseleek)

 Autumn Joy Sedum

 Cooper's Ice Plant

 Graptopetalum Ghost Plant

Box A

Box B

TRY THIS:

More and More Succulents

One of the most fun things about succulents is that they are incredibly easy to propagate. Hens and chicks practically beg to be re-potted and since they're so hardy, they can be used in various crafts and succulent arrangements.

Propagating

To propagate other succulents in your garden that don't produce offsets, simply cut off a piece of the succulent just above a leaf on the stem. Let it dry out for about three days so that the bottom has a chance to scab over. Stick the cutting into a new pot and water as you would a full-grown succulent. It should develop roots and begin to grow in around three weeks.

TRY THIS:

Succulent Container Ideas

Vintage bowl or teacup

Browse thrift stores or antique stores and find a great bowl that matches your decor style. Or use an old mug or teacup that you no longer need. Arrange succulent cuttings in the bowl in light soil that won't retain too much moisture. Use as a centerpiece on your coffee or kitchen table. Remember to keep watering to a minimum as this bowl won't have drainage holes.

Clear terrarium

Use a terrarium or empty fish bowl to create an eye catching succulent display that still allows light and air to shine through.

Bird bath or wheelbarrow

Since succulents spread so quickly, fill a bird bath or old wheelbarrow in your garden with soil and fill it with cuttings. They will soon fill the available space and trail over the edges for a unique garden attraction.

Beautiful Bouquet Garden

Cut flowers are a wonderful way to bring in a little cheer and brighten up your home. But who wants to buy overpriced grocery store bouquets every week? Growing your own vibrant, long-lasting annuals is a great way to enjoy fresh flowers...without the hefty price tag.

Bed Type: 1'x4' plus 1'x4'

Planting Boxes: 8

Plants:

 Gomphrena 'Fireworks'

 Corn Poppies

 Cornflowers

 Arrow Snapdragons

 Spray Carnations

 Zinnias

Box A

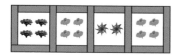

Box B

TRY THIS:

Make Cut Flowers Last Longer

Check out these tips to increase the lifespan of your cut flowers.

- Thoroughly rinse out your vase or jar with dish soap and hot water. Wipe out with a vinegar soaked paper towel to eradicate any remaining bacteria.
- Add a teaspoon of sugar and 2 teaspoons of bleach to your vase, then fill with tepid water. This will help reduce any bacteria that could cause flowers to prematurely wilt and the sugar will help feed the stems to preserve bloom color.
- Trim stems at a 45 degree angle and submerge in water right away.
- Remove any leaves or foliage that is touching the water.
- Change vase water and trim the stems again at a 45 degree angle every other day to keep flowers fresh.

Sizzling Stir Fry Garden

Grab your skillet and some soy sauce because this garden will make you want to serve yummy, sizzling stir fry for every weeknight dinner. Enjoy cooking up a healthy, veggie feast with peppers, onions, carrots, and crisp broccoli.

Bed Type: 1'x6' plus 1'x6'

Planting Boxes: 12

Plants:

 Red Beard Scallions

 Bell peppers

 Calabrese Broccoli

 Sugar Snap Peas

 Scarlet Nantes Carrots

 Silverskin Garlic

 Storage Onions

Box A

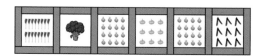

Box B

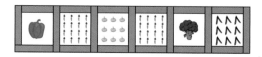

TRY THIS:

Ultimate Stir Fry

Can you say yummy? This stir fry recipe is oozing with goodness from your garden.

Ingredients:

4 cloves garlic, minced

1 Tbsp fresh ginger, minced

1 pound boneless, skinless chicken breasts, cut into ½" pieces

1 medium onion, diced

2 cups sliced carrots

1 bell pepper, seeded and sliced into thin strips

2 cups sugar snap peas

2 cups broccoli florets

Scallions, for garnish

1 tablespoon + 1 teaspoon coconut oil, divided

1/2 cup low sodium chicken broth or water

1/2 cup (gluten free) soy sauce

4 tablespoons honey

2 teaspoons cornstarch

Salt and pepper to taste

1   Heat 1 tsp coconut oil in large pan over medium heat.

2   Add vegetables and cook until tender, about five minutes.

3   Remove vegetables from pan and place in a bowl. Cover to keep in heat.

4   Turn heat to high and add remaining oil to pan.

5   Season chicken pieces with salt and pepper. Add to pan in a single layer.

6   Cook for about 4 minutes on each side or until golden brown and cooked through.

7   Return vegetables to the pan and cook for about 2 minutes to reheat.

8   Whisk together honey, chicken broth, and soy sauce in a bowl.

9   Add 1 Tbsp cold water to cornstarch and mix together in a small bowl.

10   Add garlic to the chicken and cook for 30 seconds.

11   Pour soy sauce mixture over vegetables and chicken and cook for 30 seconds.

12   Stir in cornstarch and bring to a boil. Cook until sauce has just started to thicken. About 2 minutes.

13   Serve immediately with rice and garnish with scallions. Enjoy!

Aromatic Garden

Intoxicating jasmine, sweet honeysuckle, scented geranium, and woody rosemary will have you making up excuses to walk past this garden just to inhale the heady fragrance. Utilize the vines to create a privacy screen or liven up a boring fence and include rosemary and geranium in your culinary escapades.

Bed Type: 1'x2' plus 1'x2'

Planting Boxes: 4

Plants:

 Common Honeysuckle

 Scented Geraniums

 White Rosemary

 Common Jasmine

Box A

Box B

TRY THIS:

Fresh and Fancy Floral Fragrance

Make your very own personalized perfume right at home with your fresh honeysuckle or jasmine blooms. This simple recipe is a great way to get your feet wet in the world of perfume making. All you need is water and flower petals!

What you'll need:

1 ½ cups freshly picked flowers, chopped

Cheesecloth

2 cups distilled water

Washed and sterilized small, darkly colored bottle with an airtight lid

Small saucepan

What to do:

1   Gently rinse the flower petals to remove any dirt or bugs.

2   Place petals into the small saucepan with distilled water and bring to a boil over medium heat.

3   Turn heat to low and let simmer for 2 hours.

4   Let it cool and then strain the perfume through the cheesecloth, making sure to squeeze any remaining liquid out of the flowers.

5   Transfer to the bottle and store for up to 1 month.

Hint: Harvest flowers in the morning for the strongest scent.

Lemonade Garden

Squeeze lemons from the store and create a unique lemonade twist with these delicious ingredients. Hint: If you're lucky enough to live in a warm climate where citrus can be grown, then place a dwarf lemon tree in a pot near this garden for fresh lemons to use as a garnish or juice.

Bed Type: 1'x4' plus 1'x4'

Planting Boxes: 8

Plants:

 Sunshine Blue Dwarf Blueberries

 Stevia

 Pineapple Sage

 Lemon Balm

 Honeoye Strawberries

 English Lavender

Box A

Box B

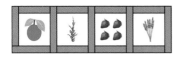

TRY THIS:

Fresh Lemonade

There is nothing quite so tasty on a warm summer day than a glass of lemonade. Skip the store-bought and make your own using fresh ingredients from your very own garden

Ingredients:

15 large strawberries, stemmed

2 cups of water

¾ cup freshly squeezed lemon juice

5 cups of water

Fresh stevia leaves to taste

Instructions:

1   Combine lemon juice, 2 cups water, and strawberries in a high-speed blender. Blend until strawberries are liquified.

2   Taste mixture to determine sweetness and then add stevia leaves as needed. Blending and tasting after every two leaves.

3   Strain through a fine sieve or cheesecloth and chill before serving over ice.

Blueberry Lemon Twist

Ingredients:

3 cups fresh blueberries

1/3 cup honey

1 cup freshly squeezed lemon juice

5-6 cups water, divided

Blueberries and lemon slices for
  garnish

Instructions:

1   Add one cup water to a small saucepan over medium heat and bring to boil. Whisk in honey until completely dissolved. Remove from heat and allow to cool.

2   Add lemon juice, 1 cup water, and blueberries to a blender and blend until totally smooth.

3   Strain through a fine sieve or cheesecloth to remove any chunks.

4   Stir in honey mixture and the remaining 3 cups of water.

5   Chill and serve over ice.

Spice Garden

Take the spice cabinet outdoors with this versatile collection. Coriander, dill, paprika, mustard, fenugreek and cumin will fill your exotic culinary ambitions and encourage you to new heights in the kitchen.

Bed Type: 1'x4' plus 1'x4'

Planting Boxes: 8

Plants:

 Santo Coriander

 Kalocsai Paprika

 Mustard

 Mammoth Dill

 Cumin

 Fenugreek

Box A

Box B

TRY THIS:

Know Your Spices

Reap all the benefits of your spice garden by learning how to best use them.

Coriander flavor profile: Coriander has a light citrusy taste that is underlaid by a raw, earthy fragrance. It also has slight hints of butter and thyme which makes it incredibly versatile in the kitchen. Use with hot peppers or even in desserts for exciting new flavors. It is also used in many Latin-American, Mexican, and Indian dishes.

Paprika flavor profile: Paprika is a mild spice with a delectable smoky flavor that is enhanced when peppers are dried over an open flame or roasted in the oven. It is often overlooked but can truly transform a dish when combined with the right ingredients. Use it in tomato-based sauces for a flavor kick or as a dry rub for various meats such as chicken, steak, and fish.

Mustard seed flavor profile: The flavor of mustard seeds differ depending on the variety grown. For instance, yellow mustard seeds (the most common) have a more mild, mellow taste, while brown and black seeds are usually more spicy and bold. Use when picking or brining or even to make your own homemade mustard.

Dill flavor profile: Dill seed is usually more intense than dill leaves and the leaves have a more lemony flavor similar to anise or parsley. The seed should be used in recipes that would benefit from a stronger dill flavor such as pickles, salad dressings, vinegars, and sauces or in mayonnaise or sour cream based sauces and dips.

Cumin flavor profile: Cumin is one of the most popular spices available with good reason. It is earthy, warm, and a signature spice in Mexican and Middle Eastern dishes. It is incredibly versatile and can be used to enhance the savory flavor of beef, lamb, and various vegetables.

Fenugreek flavor profile: Fenugreek has an interesting taste that is brought out by certain ingredients. It pairs well with vegetables, or meat like chicken and pork but could turn bitter if used excessively. Its slightly sweet, nutty flavor is often described as a cross between celery and maple.

Magical Moonlight Garden

Who says gardens can only be enjoyed during the day? This highly fragranced garden is full of voracious night bloomers that fill the evening air with their sweet perfume. Plant a night garden to maximize your time surrounded by exquisite flowers.

Bed Type: 1'x2' plus 1'x2'

Planting Boxes: 4

Plants:

 Night Phlox

 Moonflower

 Nicotiana

 4 O'Clocks

Box A

Box B

TRY THIS:

An Evening Oasis

Turn your moon garden into an evening oasis with these easy additions.

Add a place to sit

On warm summer evenings you'll want to have a comfy chair to sit and enjoy the sweet fragrance of your moon garden. If you don't already have seating on your patio, consider a porch swing, wicker couch, or hammock.

Lighting

While this garden is best experienced in the soft light of the moon, you still want to be able to see your flowers on those particularly cloudy, dark nights. Install soft lighting such as strand fairy lights, a few candles, or lanterns to set the mood.

Water feature

Moon gardens are all about serenity and unwinding from the craziness of life. What better way to relax than with the soothing sounds of a trickling water feature? Consider a small, enclosed waterfall, pond, or fountain. This will create a truly magical atmosphere and also provide a water source for bees, butterflies, hummingbirds, and other beneficial garden wildlife.

Power Smoothie Garden

Breakfast is an important meal that is often skipped in your rush to get out the door. Instead of claiming that you just "don't have time," grab your blender and whip up power smoothies with these nutrient packed ingredients from your very own garden. You won't even have to worry about going to the store!

Bed Type: 1'x4' plus 1'x4'

Planting Boxes: 8

Plants:

 Semi-Savoy Spinach

 Red Russian Kale

 Detroit Dark Red Beets

 Raspberry Shortcake

 Allstar Strawberry

 Blueberry 'Top Hat'

Box A

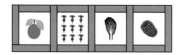

Box B

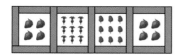

TRY THIS:

Supercharged Smoothies

For breakfast, lunch or anytime you need a boost, these smoothies deliver big taste and pack a hearty nutritional punch.

Red Ruby Power Smoothie

Beets have a great natural sweetness that makes them a perfect choice for smoothies. Plus, they are loaded with beneficial nutrients including folate, potassium, vitamin C, and they are incredibly rich in fiber. Not to mention the combined antioxidant power of beets and blueberries!

Ingredients:

- 1/2 cup unsweetened almond milk
- 1 cup mixed frozen berries (use the frozen strawberries, blueberries, and raspberries from your garden)
- 1 small beet, peeled and diced
- 1/4 cup frozen pineapple
- 1/4 cup plain Greek yogurt
- 1-2 tsp honey, optional
- 1 tsp chia seeds

Add all ingredients to a high speed blender and blend until smooth. Enjoy immediately!

Green Machine Superfood Smoothie

There's a reason green smoothies are so popular. Enjoy this superfood explosion for your daily dose of iron, potassium, and vitamin K. Green smoothies can be a little off-putting at first, but once you get over the color, you'll fall in love with the taste.

Ingredients:

1 frozen banana

2 cups unsweetened almond or coconut milk

1 cup kale, loosely packed

1 cup spinach, loosely packed

1 cup frozen berries or other frozen fruit of your choice

Blend together until smooth and enjoy!

Tip: Freeze any leftover fruit or vegetables in pre-packed smoothie bags. Simply add milk or water and blend!

Sweet Shade Garden

If you're tired of seeing "full sun" listed on the pot of every plant in the nursery and every packet of seeds, this flowering shade garden will put an end to your frustrations. The classic, timeless impatiens, the beautifully variegated coleus, delicate sapphire browallia, and intriguing fuchsia will create a spectacular display of vibrant blooms and showy foliage that thrive in the shadows.

Bed Type: 1'x2'

Planting Boxes: 2

Plants:

 New Guinea Impatiens

 Coleus 'Watermelon'

 Troll Series Browallia

 Fuchsia 'Dollar Princess'

Box A

Box B

TRY THIS:

Creating Shade

If you want to enjoy the beauty of a shade garden but don't have any natural shade, consider creating your own shade.

- Use shade cloths to creative an attractive shady spot for your box garden.

- Use a gazebo or an arbor to create a shady spot.

- Place shade umbrellas strategically around your box garden to create just the right amount of protection from the sun.

- Attach old bed sheets or curtains to posts to create a whimsical shade house for your garden.

Butterfly Kisses Garden

When it comes to butterflies, it's all about the color. Forget boring green foliage and subtle blooms, butterflies love plants that put on a show and know how to make a statement... just like them. This burst of rainbow-hued flowers is sure to attract their attention and make your patio a butterfly paradise.

Bed Type: 1'x6' plus 1'x6'

Planting Boxes: 12

Plants:

 Trailing Lantana

 'Cosmic Orange' Cosmos

 Sweet Alyssum

 'Blue Spark' Cascadia Petunias

 Ageratum

 Penta

 'Lanai' Verbena

 Toto Black Eyed Susan

Box A

Box B

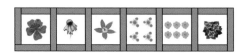

TRY THIS:

Bring on the Pollinators

Creating an oasis for hardworking pollinators is one of the easiest ways that you can contribute to the ecosystem and support essential wildlife. Other than planting this spectacularly-hued butterfly garden, try these easy ways to support and attract your delicate flying friends.

Eliminate pesticides

Chemical pesticides are one of the greatest threats of the future of butterflies and other pollinators. Besides the obvious health reasons to steer clear of harmful chemicals, you could potentially be endangering any butterflies that would alight upon your flowers. Pesticides can disrupt the fragile ecosystem of your yard and kill essential microorganisms. Simply using more natural options for pest control is an easy way to make your garden more butterfly-friendly.

Provide water

As with all living things, butterflies need water. Keep a shallow dish of water or a moist sand or mud puddle near your blooming flowers so that they will have something to drink.

Wind protection

Wind is one of the butterflies greatest enemies and can easily blow them off course. If you live in an area subject to breezy spring and summer seasons, consider placing your butterfly garden near some type of windbreak. This could be a fence, hedgerow, or house.

Places to rest

Butterflies love to sit on flat surfaces such as stones in the sun to rest and bask in the warmth. Add a few large, flat rocks to your garden. These will make excellent locations to observe butterflies at rest and get some amazing pictures.

Sensory Garden

Engage your eyes with striking roses, intrigue your sensitive fingertips with playful artemisia, breathe in the spicy-sweet scent of stock blooms, and taste the powerful flavor of fresh thyme. Install a water feature or play soothing music to finish it off and create the ultimate serene sensory experience.

Bed Type: 1'x2' plus 1'x2'

Planting Boxes: 4

Plants:

 Rainbow Sunblaze Miniature Rose

 Silver Mound Artemisia

 'Legacy' Stock

 Lemon Thyme

Box A

Box B

TRY THIS:

The Joy of a Sensory Garden

Enjoy spending time in your sensory garden to awaken your senses and clear your mind. Sit outside and read a book while you enjoy the invigorating scent of fresh stock blooms. Gift a bouquet of beautiful sunblaze roses to a friend or loved one just to show you care. Snip some thyme and try a new dish in the kitchen, whipping up your own gourmet dinner. Feel the unique texture of silver mound artemisia as you tend your garden and get reconnected with nature. Also, these plants pair wonderfully for an exquisite and unique cut flower arrangement that engages all of the senses.

Asian Cuisine Garden

If you're an experienced cook who likes to venture away from traditional vegetables like carrots, and tomatoes, this garden is for you. Whip up your favorite Asian cuisine recipes or enjoy the distinctive flavors of these easy-to-grow palate expanding veggies by themselves.

Bed Type: 1'x4' plus 1'x4'

Planting Boxes: 8

Plants:

 'Joi Choi' Bok Choy

 'Agate' Edamame

 'Spring Light' Daikon Radish

 Lemongrass

 Chinese Broccoli

 Gai Choy Mustard Greens

Box A

Box B

TRY THIS:

Prepare for Taste

Try these easy ways to prepare your veggies for simple side dishes or delicious additions to your main meal.

- Boil edamame pods in water for five minutes and sprinkle with coarse salt. Simply pop the delicious beans right into your mouth while warm.
- Sautee chinese broccoli with ginger, garlic, soy sauce, and oyster sauce.
- Fresh lemongrass adds a tangy citrus flavor to soups and Asian salads.
- Enjoy raw bok choy with a vegetable dip or slice up for a salad.
- Cook mustard greens with garlic, soy sauce, rice wine vinegar, sake, and honey. Don't forget to top with toasted sesame seeds!
- Boil daikon in stews, soups or add to stir fry. Or lightly steam and serve with olive oil, salt, and lemon juice.

Nothing But Peppers Garden

Who doesn't love peppers? This colorful garden has every pepper you'll need to meet aesthetic and culinary needs. Red hot, sweet orange, purple beauties, and the classic jalapeño. Soon you'll be enjoying peppers at every meal. And don't forget about that midafternoon snack!

Bed Type: 1'x2' plus 1'x2'

Planting Boxes: 4

Plants:

 Jalapeño Peppers

 Orange Lunchbox Sweet Snacking Pepper

 Thai Hot Pepper

 Oda Pepper

Box A

Box B

TRY THIS:

Know Your Peppers

Jalapeño: One of the most common peppers, along with bell peppers, jalapeños are a staple in the kitchen and a great choice when you need to add a little heat to any savory dish. Use as a pizza or taco topping, pickle and save for later, or make yummy appetizers or salsa.

Lunchbox Sweet Snacking: The name says it all, really. These are the ultimate sweet snacking peppers and are delicious when eaten raw straight off the plant. Chill in the fridge for an even better crunch and serve with your favorite dip. Kids love them too!

Thai hot: This gorgeous pepper plant has striking ornamental value, but also produces peppers with outstanding flavor. Thai peppers are significantly hotter than jalapeños but not quite as hot as habaneros, so keep that frame of reference in mind when you are cooking with them. Naturally, many Thai and Asian recipes call for these peppers to add a little kick to vegetable and meat dishes.

Oda: The bright purple peppers are great for stir fry, sauce, salads or as a raw snack. Oda peppers have a similar flavor to bell peppers, but bring a whole new element to any dish with their spectacular color and unique taste.

ARE YOU READY TO BOX GARDEN?

I hope that *The Instant Box Garden Miracle* has inspired you to create your very own box garden or maybe many box gardens. Don't let a lack of space or being new to gardening keep you from enjoying all that box gardens have to offer. They are a perfect anytime project and a great way to get the whole family involved in growing beautiful flowers and food gardens.

Above all, have fun and grow well!

SUSAN PATTERSON, MASTER GARDENER

PLANTING AND HARVESTING GUIDE

Below you will find all the plants used to make the gardens outlined in this book. Specific varieties are listed only where planting and harvesting specifics are essential.

Ageratum

- **Starting:** Start seeds indoors eight to ten weeks before the last expected frost date. The seeds need light to germinate so simply press lightly into soil.

- **Planting:** Place seedlings in the garden after all danger of frost has passed. 4 per sq. ft.

- **Harvest:** Flowers will bloom throughout the summer with consistent deadheading.

- **Tips:** Pinch back the tips of young plants to encourage bushier growth and a more full plant.

- **Consider this:** Spider mites can attack ageratum during hot, dry spells in the summertime. Mist plants with water to deter spider mites as they don't like humidity.

Allstar Strawberry

- **Planting:** Transplant small plants into garden a few weeks before last frost date. 4 plants per sq. ft.

- **Harvest:** Berries will be ready to harvest around 30 days after the flowers bloom. Fruit should be bright red and firm.

- **Tips:** Allstar strawberries will produce one large crop in midsummer. Harvest and freeze the berries to enjoy delicious smoothies all year long.

- **Consider this:** Don't bury the crown of the strawberry plant as leaves and fruit develop there. Just plant the roots and keep the crown level with the soil surface.

Alpine Strawberry

- **Planting:** Transplant small plants into garden a few weeks before the last frost date. 1 plant per sq. ft.

- **Harvest:** Berries will be ready to harvest around 30 days after flowers bloom and will produce fruit all season long.

- **Tips:** Birds absolutely love strawberries. Protect your plants with lightweight bird netting as the berries ripen.

- **Consider this:** Alpine strawberries are heavy feeders. Provide lots of well-rotted compost to the garden before planting for the healthiest plants.

Alyssum

- **Starting:** Start seeds indoors eight to ten weeks before the last expected frost date. Simply press lightly into soil.

- **Planting:** Transplant into garden after last frost. 4 per sq. ft.

- **Harvest:** Butterflies love the honey-like fragrance of the alyssum flower.

- **Tips:** Alyssum is incredibly heat and drought tolerant but make sure not to overwater. Plants may get Botrytis blight when grown in overly wet areas.

- **Consider this:** Trim back the stems by ⅓ after blooming to get a second wave of beautiful flowers.

Artemisia

- **Planting:** Transplant small plants into garden after all danger of frost has passed. 1 per sq. ft.

- **Harvest:** Silver mound artemisia practically begs to be stroked. Run your hand along its soft foliage for an intriguing sensory experience.

- **Tips:** Grows in a mound and rarely needs dividing. In fact, it is best left alone as it thrives on benign neglect.

- **Consider this:** Prune back to 5" in late fall to clean up spent foliage and make room for new growth.

Arugula

- **Planting:** Plant seeds 1/4" deep directly into the garden four weeks before the last expected frost date. Broadcast seeds (hand scatter) and thin to 9 per sq. ft.

- **Harvest:** 21-30 days for full size leaves.

- **Tips:** Plant a new crop every three weeks until midsummer to maximize yield and prevent flower production.

- **Warning:** Arugula is a cool season crop so it is important to provide shade to keep it cool throughout the summer.

Baby's Breath

- **Planting:** Sow seeds ¼" directly into the garden after the danger of heavy frost has passed. Transplant into garden after last frost. 6 per sq. ft. Thin to one hearty plant once plants are 1" tall.

- **Harvest:** Cut long stems after the morning dew has dried. Wait to harvest until the buds start to open.

- **Tips:** Remove foliage and hang bundles upside down to dry for two to three weeks.

- **Consider this:** Low baby's breath is not considered invasive since it is an annual and must be replanted each year.

Banana Pepper

- **Starting:** Start seeds indoors ¼" deep, twelve weeks before the last expected frost date.

- **Planting:** Transplant into garden when soil reaches 65 degrees F or two weeks after last frost. 1 per sq. ft.

- **Harvest:** 70 days to full maturity. More mature peppers will have better flavor.

- **Tips:** Use pruning shears or a sharp knife to harvest peppers with some stem still attached as pulling them off can cause damage to the plant.

- **Consider this:** Ripe rot can occur when peppers are kept in a warm, humid environment as they ripen. Store harvested peppers in fridge or freezer to prevent this from developing.

Basil

- **Starting:** Start seeds indoors ¼" deep, six weeks before the last expected frost date

- **Planting:** Transplant into garden when soil reaches 70 degrees F or two weeks after last frost. 2 plants per sq. ft.

- **Harvest:** 40-55 days to maturity. Harvest sprigs as needed. Collect leaves in early morning when flavor will be strongest.

- **Tips:** Pinch stems often to improve flavor and growth. Never cut the woody part of the stem or basil won't grow back. Basil hates cold weather, harvest your whole plant if temperatures are predicted to drop or frost is imminent.

- **Consider this:** Poor drainage is the greatest threat to basil. Make sure that it is not sitting in water. About six weeks after planting in the garden, pinch off the center shoot to prevent early flowering. Cut off any flowers that do grow.

Beets

- **Planting:** Plant beet seeds ½" deep directly into the garden as soon as the soil can be worked in the spring. Once seeds have germinated, thin to 9 per sq. ft.

- **Harvest:** 40-60 days to maturity. Harvest once beets have reached desired size. Young beets will be more tender. Enjoy the baby greens from the thinned seedlings in salads.

- **Tips:** Soak seeds in warm water overnight to speed germination.

- **Consider this:** Beets can be stored for up to one month in the fridge. Trim off leaves (leaving about ½"), brush off loose soil, and store in a plastic bag in the veggie drawer.

Bell Pepper

- **Starting:** Start seeds indoors ¼" deep, twelve weeks before the last expected frost date.

- **Planting:** Transplant into garden when soil reaches 65 degrees F or two weeks after last frost. 1 per sq. ft.

- **Harvest:** 65-85 days to full maturity. More mature peppers will have better flavor.

- **Tips:** Pinch off early blossoms to encourage larger peppers and a higher yield. Provide cone-shaped tomato cages if you notice that the plant is drooping.

- **Consider this:** Ripe rot can occur when peppers are kept in a warm, humid environment as they ripen. Avoid planting peppers in soil where you've recently grown other members: tomatoes, potatoes, or eggplants since this can expose peppers to disease. Store harvested peppers in fridge or freezer to prevent this from happening.

Black Beans

- **Planting:** Plant seeds directly in the garden around the last frost when soil has warmed to about 60 degrees F. 6 plants per sq. ft. Soak seeds overnight before planting.

- **Harvest:** Leave beans on the vine until fall to allow them to dry. Pods are ready for harvest when beans rattle.

- **Tips:** Collect dry bean pods and put them in a pillowcase or bag. Hit pillowcase against the ground or stomp on it to encourage seed pods to break apart. You can open seed pods by hand.

- **Consider this:** Before putting seeds into an airtight container to store until next season, test a bean with your fingernail. If it leaves a dent, allow seeds to dry for a few more weeks.

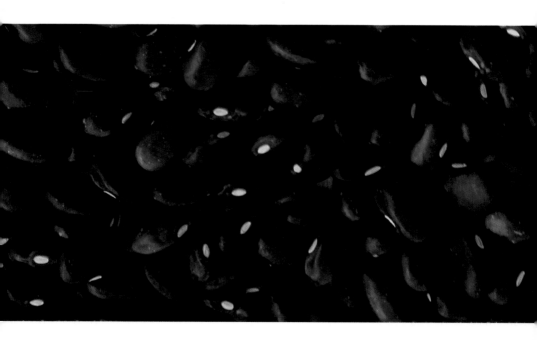

Black Eyed Susan

- **Planting:** Plant seeds directly outdoors ¼" deep after all danger of frost has passed and when soil reaches 70 degrees F. 1 per sq. ft. Perennial in zones 3-9.

- **Harvest:** Blooms readily from early summer to the first frost.

- **Tips:** Divide as needed in the following years to spread the love and keep plants from overtaking your garden.

- **Consider this:** Black eyed susans make lovely cut flowers as well and can last for up to 10 days in an arrangement.

Blueberry

- **Planting:** Plant small transplants directly into garden in hole twice the size of the root ball. Plant in early spring as soon as the ground can be worked. Hardy in zones 5-10. 1 per sq. ft.

- **Harvest:** Harvest berries when they reach desired ripeness.

- **Tips:** After the first year, prune branches in early spring before blossoms develop.

- **Consider this:** Brown leaves could be a sign of too little water. Make sure to keep your blueberry bush hydrated.

Bok Choy

- **Starting:** Start seeds indoors ¼" deep, four to six weeks before the last expected frost date.

- **Planting:** Transplant into garden one to two weeks before the last expected frost date or when nighttime temperatures are above 50 degrees F. 4 per sq. ft.

- **Harvest:** 45-50 days to maturity. It should be around 12"-18" tall.

- **Tips:** Be sure to harvest before the weather warms to prevent bok choy from going to seed.

- **Consider this:** Cut back plants about an inch above the ground and you may be able to get a second harvest.

Brandywine and Roma Tomato

- **Starting:** Start seeds indoors ¼" deep, eight weeks before the last expected frost date.

- **Planting:** Transplant into garden when soil reaches 65 degrees F or two weeks after last frost. 1 per sq. ft.

- **Harvest:** 75 days to maturity.

- **Tips:** Provide a trellis or tomato cage to support the vines and maximize space.

- **Consider this:** Sunscald is UV damage to the outer layer of the plant and can diminish flavor and cause unsightly patches on tomatoes. Let foliage grow to cover and protect fruit.

Broccoli

- **Starting:** Start seeds indoors ¼" deep, six weeks before the last expected frost date.

- **Planting:** Transplant into garden when seedlings have two sets of leaves. 1 per sq. ft.

- **Harvest:** 50-70 days to full maturity from transplant. Use a sharp knife and cut the stem at an angle right below the crown to harvest.

- **Tips:** Side shoots will keep producing several weeks after you harvest the main head. Enjoy these when they are still tight and green.

- **Consider this:** Erect a shade cloth to protect broccoli from direct afternoon sun. Cover the young seedlings with landscape fabric for the first few weeks after transplant to protect from flea beetles and cabbage worm.

Browallia

- **Starting:** Start seeds indoors by lightly pressing into the growing medium, eight to ten weeks before the last expected frost date.

- **Planting:** Transplant into garden once soil warms and all danger of frost has passed. Seedlings should have at least two sets of true leaves. 1 per sq. ft.

- **Harvest:** Blooms from spring until the end of summer.

- **Tips:** Protect seedlings from slugs and cutworms with a toilet paper roll collar. Remove when seedlings have become established.

- **Consider this:** Be sure to keep the soil moist throughout the growing season.

Bush Beans

- **Planting:** Plant seeds 1 ½ " deep in the garden as soon as the ground has warmed a bit in the spring. Soil should be a minimum of 65 degrees F.

- **Harvest:** Harvest before pods are not quite mature and still tender. This is usually one to two weeks after flowering. Pick beans often to keep the plants producing.

- **Tips:** Help bush beans germinate by soaking them overnight before planting. Plant immediately after soaking to avoid rot.

- **Consider this:** Beans like a lot of mulch, it helps keep them hydrated. Provide a generous layer of straw or other mulch around plants.

Calendula

- **Starting:** Start seeds indoors ¼" deep, six to eight weeks before the last expected frost date.

- **Planting:** Transplant seedlings into garden after last frost. 2 per sq. ft.

- **Harvest:** 45-60 days from seed to flower. Cut off flower heads as soon as they bloom in late morning. Dry on a flat screen or other surface right away.

- **Tips:** Store in an airtight jar or container in a cool, dark place, once completely dry.

- **Consider this:** Calendula is susceptible to powdery mildew. Make sure to allow appropriate air circulation around the plant to prevent moisture from collecting.

Carnation

- **Starting:** Start seeds indoors, six to eight weeks before the last expected frost date. Cover seeds with a light layer of soil.

- **Planting:** Transplant into garden after the last expected frost date when seedlings are about four inches tall. 1 per sq. ft.

- **Harvest:** Cut carnation stems once blooms are open. Continue pinching off any spent blooms or leaves to encourage new growth.

- **Tips:** Stake any stems that are falling over or drooping. Provide adequate air circulation between plants to prevent mold and mildew from trapped humidity.

- **Consider this:** Carnations are the ultimate cut flower and can last for 2-3 weeks in a vase with proper care.

Carrots

- **Planting:** Sow seeds ¼" deep directly into the garden three weeks before the last expected frost date. Plant 30 seeds per sq. ft. and thin to 16 once seedlings have started to pop up.

- **Harvest:** 55 days to maturity. Dig around the carrots with a small trowel to loosen the dirt and harvest, or merely pluck them gently out of the ground by the green foliage.

- **Tips:** Consistent moisture will produce tasty carrots. Keep soil damp for optimal flavor. Your kiddos will love pulling up the sweet, orange bounty. Give the veggies a quick rinse and even the most picky eater will be gobbling up their homegrown carrots.

- **Consider this:** Root tops that are exposed to sunlight may turn green and become inedible. Consistent moisture will produce tasty carrots. Keep soil damp for optimal flavor. Be sure to cover any peek-a-boo carrots with mulch or soil. Experiment with different varieties and colors. Purple carrots are sure to please!

Celosia

- **Starting:** Start seeds indoors ¼" deep, four weeks before the last expected frost date.

- **Planting:** Transplant into garden when plants are at least four inches tall. 4 per sq. ft.

- **Harvest:** Harvest when flowers are almost fully open.

- **Tips:** Tie together with a rubber band and dry in a cool, dark, location for about one month.

- **Consider this:** Celosia are incredibly sensitive to cold weather so don't rush to get in the ground early in the season. They are fast growers and will still produce beautiful blooms even if planted in late spring.

Chamomile

- **Starting:** Start seeds indoors, six weeks before the last expected frost date. Scatter seeds on starting area and simply press firmly into the soil. The seeds need light to germinate so don't cover them with soil.

- **Planting:** Transplant seedlings into the garden after last frost. 4 plants per sq. ft.

- **Harvest:** 30 days to maturity. Harvest flowers as desired.

- **Tips:** Chamomile is a fairly disease and pest resistant plant and can actually be grown near cucumbers to help deter unwanted bugs.

- **Consider this:** Chamomile will self seed and your patch will keep growing every year. You can also collect seeds and replant them in other areas of the garden.

Cherry Tomato

- **Starting:** Start seeds indoors ¼" deep, eight to ten weeks before the last expected frost date.

- **Planting:** Transplant into garden when soil reaches 65 degrees or two weeks after last frost. 1 per sq. ft.

- **Harvest:** 65-70 days to maturity.

- **Tips:** Provide a cage for support.

- **Consider this:** Cherry tomatoes can easily develop cracks. Keep moisture levels even throughout the growing season.

Chinese Broccoli

- **Planting:** Plant seeds directly in the garden as soon as soil can be worked. Thin to 2 per sq. ft. once plants are 3" tall.

- **Harvest:** 60-70 days to full maturity. Harvest stems and leaves as soon as the first flowers appear.

- **Tips:** Cut the stalks about 8" above the base of the plant for continual harvest.

- **Consider this:** Powdery mildew could be a problem in a warm, humid environment. Make sure to provide adequate airflow around plants.

Chocolate Mint

- **Planting:** Transplant small plants into garden after last frost. Keep the mint in the pot and bury the pot. This will keep the mint from taking over your garden. 1 plant per sq. ft.

- **Harvest:** Harvest leaves and stems as desired.

- **Tips:** Mint is a perennial in most climates and will last for years. Simply lift and replant the pot every three to four years to keep the flavor and scent strong.

- **Consider this:** Be sure to contain the mint by burying it in a pot in the raised bed.

Cilantro

- **Planting:** Plant seeds ¼" - ½" deep directly into the garden around last frost date. Sow 18 seeds per sq. ft. and thin to 9 plants per sq. ft.

- **Harvest:** 21-28 days to full maturity. Cilantro can be harvested continually until it goes to seed.

- **Tips:** Cilantro goes to seed quickly. Harvest and plant more seeds about every three weeks to keep up a good supply or plant more tomatoes where the cilantro was. Thin plants properly to allow air circulation and prevent powdery mildew.

- **Consider this:** If you live in a hot climate, be sure to provide light shade as warmer weather tends to cause cilantro to bolt. In addition, consider buying a slow bolt variety of cilantro. Snip off the top part of the main cilantro stem as soon as it begins to develop flower buds. This redirects the energy and nutrients into leaf production, not flower or seed growth.

Coleus

- **Starting:** Start seeds indoors on the surface of the growing medium, eight to ten weeks before the last expected frost date.

- **Planting:** Transplant into garden after all danger of frost has passed and evening temperatures reach 60 degrees F. 1 per sq. ft.

- **Harvest:** Enjoy vibrant foliage through the warm season and then propagate shoots from cuttings and keep as houseplants until the following spring.

- **Tips:** Pinch back the shoots of the plants in early summer to encourage fuller growth.

- **Consider this:** Coleus is incredibly easy to propagate. Simply stick a cutting in a glass of water, wait until it has roots and place it in a pot. Now you have another coleus plant to share or place in your garden.

Coriander

- **Planting:** Plant cilantro seeds ¼ to ½" deep directly into the garden around last frost date. Sow 18 seeds per sq. ft. and thin to 9 plants per sq. ft.

- **Harvest:** To harvest coriander seeds from cilantro plants, let the plant bolt and go to flower. Wait until seed heads form and then collect seeds and dry.

- **Tips:** Collect stems with seed heads and tie together in a paper bag with stems sticking out. Hang upside down for three weeks and shake the bag. This will leave the dry seeds at the bottom of the bag.

- **Consider this:** Coriander has a slight lemony flavor and can be ground into a powder or used as seeds. Cilantro and coriander are the same plant, but cilantro is the leafy green part, while coriander refers to the seeds it produces after it flowers.

Cornflower

- **Planting:** Sow seed directly into garden ½" deep after last frost date. Thin to 2 per sq. ft.

- **Harvest:** Cut stems before flowers open fully to encourage growth throughout the summer.

- **Tips:** Some cornflowers may require staking since they have such tall stems. Keep an eye on your plants and add support if you notice them falling over.

- **Consider this:** Not only do they make great cut flowers, cornflowers are actually edible and have a clove-like flavor and may be used in teas, cakes and rice dishes.

Cosmos

- **Planting:** Sow seeds directly in the garden after the last danger of frost by lightly pressing them into the soil. Broadcast seeds and thin seedlings to 6 per sq. ft.

- **Harvest:** Usually takes around seven weeks from seed to bloom.

- **Tips:** Comos may self seed and produce plants the following year. Collect the dried seed and plant in the garden the following spring.

- **Consider this:** May require staking in strong winds.

Cucumber

- **Starting:** Start seeds indoors 1/2" deep, three weeks before the last expected frost date.

- **Planting:** Transplant cucumbers into garden 1 per sq. ft. Sow two weeks after last frost. Plant another crop two weeks later to extend harvest.

- **Harvest:** 45-50 days to maturity. Fruits will reach only 4 inches long and should be firm and deep green.

- **Tips:** Provide a trellis to prevent cucumbers from trailing through your bed. Cucumbers can become mushy and bitter if left to get too big. Harvest often.

- **Consider this:** Cucumber beetles love to chew holes in leaves and flowers and scar stems and fruits. They also spread a disease that causes the plants to wilt and die. Keep an eye out for these bugs. Plant tansy near your cucumbers if you notice an increase in beetles as it can help repel them. Make sure to provide airflow around the plant to prevent diseases like powdery mildew and bacterial wilt.

Cumin

- **Starting:** Start seeds indoors ¼" deep six to eight weeks before the last expected frost. Soak the seeds for at least eight hours before sowing for better germination.

- **Planting:** Transplant into garden at least two weeks after last frost. 4 per sq. ft.

- **Harvest:** 120 days to seed production. Harvest seeds after the flowers bloom.

- **Tips:** Toast cumin seeds in a skillet over high heat for about 1 minute. Shake the pan constantly to prevent burning. Transfer them quickly to another container and grind to release even more flavor.

- **Consider this:** Remember, it is important to ensure that seeds are properly dried before storing to prevent mold and mildew.

Daikon Radish

- **Planting:** Start seeds ½" deep as soon as the soil can be worked in the spring. Thin to 4 per sq. ft.

- **Harvest:** 60-70 days to maturity.

- **Tips:** Loosen the surrounding soil before harvesting to prevent the root from snapping off.

- **Consider this:** Brush off the dirt (don't rinse) and store in the fridge for up to two weeks.

Dandelion

- **Starting:** Start seeds indoors ¼" deep six to eight weeks before the last frost date.

- **Planting:** Transplant seedlings after last frost, around mid-spring. 9 per sq. ft.

- **Harvest:** Harvest dandelion greens by cutting leaves off just below the crown with a sharp knife. Make sure to harvest before the plant flowers to avoid bitter greens.

- **Tips:** Eat greens fresh for medicinal benefits. Store in an airtight container in the fridge for up to two weeks.

- **Consider this:** Dandelions spread quickly and are often considered a weed. Don't let them flower to keep them from overtaking your garden.

Dill

- **Planting:** Sow seeds directly into the garden after last frost when soil is around 60-70 degrees F. Thin to 2 per sq. ft. - about two weeks after seeds sprout.

- **Harvest:** Let dill greens flower and collect flower heads when they are dry. Seeds should fall right out with a gentle shake.

- **Tips:** Place seed pods in a paper bag and shake to separate flower debris from the seeds.

- **Consider this:** If you want to use fresh dill, simply choose one plant to use for that purpose and harvest the leaves as desired. Otherwise, let plants go to seed without harvesting.

Dwarf Sunflower

- **Planting:** Sow seeds directly into garden 1" deep when soil reaches 55-60 degrees F or two weeks after the last frost date. Thin to 1 plant per sq. ft when seedlings reach 6 inches tall.

- **Harvest:** With dwarf sunflowers, merely enjoy their beauty throughout the growing season.

- **Tips:** Provide stakes and loosely tie sunflower stalks to help support their heavy blooms as the plant develops.

- **Consider this:** Don't forget to save the seeds in the fall once the blooms are spent. Collect the seeds and let your kids feed the birds or enjoy them roasted and salted as a snack.

Echinacea

- **Planting:** Sow ½" deep directly into garden when light frost is still possible. Grows as a perennial. 1 plant per sq. ft.

- **Harvest:** 90-110 days from seed to flower. Cut down the stem to the lowest leaves once echinacea flowers and dry immediately.

- **Tips:** Store in an airtight jar or container in a cool, dark place once dry.

- **Consider this:** Cut the plant back by a third in late summer to encourage fresh growth and new blooms.

Edamame

- **Planting:** Start seeds outdoors ½" deep when soil reaches 60 degrees F or two weeks after last frost. Sow more seeds every few weeks to harvest throughout the summer. Thin to 4 per sq. ft. when plants are 4" tall.

- **Harvest:** Harvest beans as soon as pods are plump and filled out. Don't wait too long or the beans will turn yellow and become bitter.

- **Tips:** All edamame beans on a single plant are ready for harvest at the same time. Cook them and eat them as soon as possible. You can also freeze the beans while still in the pods to enjoy later.

- **Consider this:** Plants may need staking in windy environments.

Fennel

- **Planting:** Sow fennel seeds directly into the garden after last frost. Thin to 1 plant per sq. ft.

- **Harvest:** Harvest leaves anytime during the growing season. The more you trim it, the bushier and fuller it will grow.

- **Tips:** Soak seeds two days before planting to encourage germination.

- **Consider this:** Parsleyworm, the larva of a black swallowtail butterfly, and looks like a green caterpillar with black and yellow bands, is a common visitor of fennel and likes to eat the foliage. Check leaves regularly, and hand-pick worms as soon as you see them.

Fenugreek

- **Planting:** Sow seeds directly into the garden ¼" deep after all danger of frost has passed. Sow densely and thin to 4 per sq. ft. once seedlings have sprouted.

- **Harvest:** 120-150 days to maturity. Plants will produce beans that contain seeds. Wait to harvest until plants begin to die.

- **Tips:** Let seeds dry in the sun before storing.

- **Consider this:** Seeds taste like maple and are often used in traditional Indian dishes such as curry and tea. The seeds alone are bitter but will elevate any existing sweet flavor.

- **Consider this:** Fenugreek is not fond of hot temperatures and does best in cool and mildly warm weather.

Feverfew

- **Starting:** Start seeds indoors six weeks before the last expected frost date by lightly tamping them into the soil. They need light to germinate so be sure not to plant them too far down.

- **Planting:** Transplant into garden when soil reaches 60 degrees F or after last frost date has passed. Usually grown as an annual but can be a perennial in warmer climates. 1 per sq. ft.

- **Harvest:** Harvest when in full flower and begin the drying process immediately.

- **Tips:** Feverfew could be considered invasive since it reseeds easily. Keep an eye out for unwanted sprouts.

- **Consider this:** The strong citrus-like scent of feverfew could repel bees so make sure not to grow it near other plants that require bees for pollination.

Four O'Clocks

- **Starting:** Start seeds indoors ¼" deep, six to eight weeks before the last expected frost. Perennial in zones 7b-11.

- **Planting:** Transplant into garden after all danger of frost has passed. 1 plant per sq. ft.

- **Harvest:** Flowers open around 4 o'clock in the afternoon and stay open till morning. Enjoy these brightly colored blooms in the cool of the evening.

- **Tips:** Seeds can easily be collected to plant other places the following season.

- **Consider this:** The 4 O'Clock opens in the early evening and heralds the delightful blooms of the rest of the moon garden.

Fuchsia

- **Planting:** Transplant small plants into garden after all danger of frost has passed. 4 per sq. ft.

- **Harvest:** Flowers will bloom consistently while weather is warm.

- **Tips:** Deadhead spent blooms frequently to encourage more flowers.

- **Consider this:** If you want to save seeds for the following year, don't deadhead flowers. Let them fall to the ground and allow seed pods to develop. Open these seed pods and rinse the seeds inside. Let dry on a flat surface for at least a week. Store in a paper bag in an airtight container for the next planting season.

Garlic

- **Planting:** Timing is essential when planting garlic. Plant six to eight weeks before the first expected fall frost date, before the ground freezes. Break apart individual garlic cloves from the head, a few days before planting but leave on the papery coating. Push clove into ground two inches deep in an upright position with the wide root side facing down and pointed end facing up. 9 per sq. ft.

- **Harvest:** Harvest when tops begin to yellow and fall over but before they are completely dry. This is usually around nine months after planting a fall crop. Carefully dig up bulbs with a spade, don't pull! Hang to cure in an airy, shady, dry spot for two weeks.

- **Tips:** Planting timing will vary depending on the climate so be sure to pay attention to your local frost predictions and weather patterns. Check stored garlic often and immediately use any heads that are showing signs of sprouting.

- **Consider this:** Once bulbs are dry, trim off any root or leaves and brush off dirt. Leave the wrappers on but remove the outer layer. Save your best formed bulbs to plant again in the fall.

Ghost Plant

- **Planting:** Start from cuttings in the spring after the last frost. Hardy in zones 7 and higher. 2 per sq. ft.

- **Harvest:** Produces small yellow flowers in the spring.

- **Tips:** Keep ghost plant trimmed to encourage a fuller shape and prevent it from getting leggy.

- **Consider this:** Ghost plant succulents will change color from yellow-pink to bluish-grey depending on the sun exposure. If you want the blue color be sure to plant them in an area with dappled shade.

Gomphrena

- **Starting:** Start seeds indoors 1/4" deep, six to eight weeks before the last expected frost date.

- **Planting:** Transplant into garden after the last expected frost date. 2 per sq. ft.

- **Harvest:** Harvest blooms for cut flowers just after they open.

- **Tips:** Gomphrenas also make beautiful dried flowers. Simply tie together any excess blooms and hang them upside down in a dry location.

- **Consider this:** May be susceptible to powdery mildew if watered on the leaves. Always water at the base of the plant to prevent excess moisture from collecting on the foliage.

Green Leaf Lettuce

- **Starting:** Start seeds indoors ¼" deep, eight weeks before the last expected frost date.

- **Planting:** Transplant into garden when seedlings are four weeks old. 4 plants per sq. ft.

- **Harvest:** 28 days for baby lettuce, 45 for mature leaves. Can be harvested any time.

- **Tips:** Provide afternoon shade in warm weather to prevent wilting and stress on the plant. A stressed plant is much more susceptible to pests and disease. Plant more lettuce every two to four weeks to keep up a good supply.

- **Consider this:** Aphids love to eat lettuce. Plant chives or garlic between your lettuce to control aphids and act as "barrier plants."

Hens and Chicks

- **Planting:** Transplant offsets or seedlings into the garden after last frost in spring. 2 plants per sq. ft.

- **Harvest:** Hens and Chicks will usually multiply by at least four during the growing season. The "hen" will send off underground roots that produce "chicks." They will spread nicely to occupy available space.

- **Tips:** The chicks (offsets) can be gently pulled away from the main plant and replanted at any time.

- **Consider this:** As with most succulents, hens and chicks will die in soggy soil. In fact, they thrive on mild neglect so be sure not to water too often.

Honeysuckle

- **Planting:** Grow from small plants after all danger of frost has passed. Perennial. 1 per. sq. ft.

- **Harvest:** Enjoy beautiful, fragrant flowers from late spring through summer.

- **Tips:** Honeysuckle is a fast-growing vine. Make sure to provide a trellis, cage, railing, or fence for it to trail along.

- **Consider this:** Prune honeysuckle vine in the late fall to keep it tamed and tidy. But only lightly prune plants until they are well-established.

Ice Plant

- **Planting:** Plant from cuttings after the last expected frost date. Perennial in zones 8-10. 1 per sq. ft.

- **Harvest:** Cuttings will grow quickly and begin to create a vibrant groundcover for your garden.

- **Tips:** The purple-toned flowers bloom regularly in proper conditions and will add a nice colorful accent to your succulent garden.

- **Consider this:** Prune slightly throughout the year to keep the trailing plant contained.

Impatiens

- **Planting:** Transplant small plants into garden after all danger of frost has passed. 4 per sq. ft.

- **Harvest:** Enjoy this shade-tolerant plant throughout the summer and then pull up once it dies back in the cold weather.

- **Tips:** Unlike other blooming annuals, impatiens don't require deadheading. They will drop their spent blooms and produce new ones.

- **Consider this:** There are many different varieties of impatiens. Choose the color and look that suits your garden best.

Jalapeño Pepper

- **Starting:** Start seeds indoors ¼" deep, 12 weeks before the last expected frost date.

- **Planting:** Transplant into garden when soil reaches 65 degrees F or two weeks after last frost. 1 per sq. ft.

- **Harvest:** 70-75 days to full maturity. Harvest when peppers are green.

- **Tips:** Picking peppers will encourage more growth and a more bountiful harvest.

- **Consider this:** Jalapeños are vulnerable to pests such as aphids, mealy bugs, and whitefly. Keep an eye out for infestation and treat with a non-toxic pest control.

Jasmine

- **Planting:** Plant a young vine in the garden after the last expected frost date. Perennial in zones 7-10. 1 per sq. ft.

- **Harvest:** Enjoy fragrant blooms throughout the summer.

- **Tips:** Train vines when they are young by winding them through the trellis or use plant ties to attach them to a fence or railing. Remove ties as the plant matures.

- **Consider this:** Prune heavily when blooms are finished in the fall to encourage new growth and keep jasmine from getting unruly.

Kale

- **Starting:** Start seeds indoors 1/2" deep, eight weeks before the last expected frost date.

- **Planting:** Transplant into garden six weeks before the last expected frost date. 1 per sq. ft.

- **Harvest:** 60 days to maturity.

- **Tips:** Kale is incredibly frost hardy and tastes even better when it is exposed to cold weather.

- **Consider this:** Kale will grow best in full sun as long as it's not too hot. Provide shade if summer temperatures soar.

Lambs Ear

- **Starting:** Start seeds indoors 1/4" deep, eight to ten weeks before the last expected frost date.

- **Planting:** Transplant into garden after the last expected frost date. Perennial. 1 per sq. ft.

- **Harvest:** Enjoy lambs ear throughout the growing season. Children can pluck leaves often to enjoy their fuzzy feel and the plant will quickly grow back.

- **Tips:** Since lambs ear is a perennial and could eventually overtake your box garden, divide it every few years to plant in other areas of your yard.

- **Consider this:** Lamb's ear can tolerate poor soil but make sure it is well draining as soggy soil will cause rot.

Lantana

- **Planting:** Plant lantana in garden when soil warms and all danger of frost has passed. 1 per sq. ft.

- **Harvest:** Many butterfly species love the nectar from lantana plants.

- **Tips:** Remove spent blooms to lengthen growing season and encourage flowering.

- **Consider this:** If you live in a warmer environment that doesn't have a winter frost, you may have to trim back leggy offshoots to prevent overgrowth.

Lavender

- **Planting:** Lavender does best when grown from small plants. Transplant into garden after last frost when temperature stays above 40 degrees F. 1 plant per sq. ft.

- **Harvest:** Harvest sprigs as needed throughout the growing season.

- **Tips:** Harvest with garden shears to preserve fragile blooms and maximize flavor. Harvest in the early morning when oils are most potent and flavor is strong.

- **Consider this:** Lavender can develop fungus if climate is humid. Trim plants to provide air circulation. Prune back lavender each spring, leaving about ⅓ of old growth.

Lemon Balm

- **Planting:** Lemon balm does best when grown from small plants. Transplant into garden after all danger of frost has passed. 1 plant per sq. ft.

- **Harvest:** Harvest sprigs as needed throughout the growing season.

- **Tips:** Though lemon balm does not spread by underground runners like mint, it will still spread seeds and begin to take over the garden if left unchecked. Trim it back to several inches tall a few times during the growing season.

- **Consider this:** Trim back most of the lemon balm any time it is beginning to look tired or leggy. Don't worry! It will grow back fuller and healthier than ever in no time.

Lemon Verbena

- **Starting:** Start seeds indoors ⅛" deep, six to eight weeks before the last expected frost date. Be patient! Seeds can take up to a month to germinate.

- **Planting:** Transplant into garden after the last frost. 2 plants per sq. ft.

- **Harvest:** Harvest leaves and stems as desired.

- **Tips:** Dry leaves on screens in a cool, dark area and store in an airtight container.

- **Consider this:** Lemon verbena can become leggy if left to roam free. Trim stems regularly to encourage a full, bushy plant with full flavor.

Lemongrass

- **Planting:** Plant lemongrass outdoors after all danger of frost has passed. 1 per sq. ft.

- **Harvest:** Harvest when plants are 12" tall and stem bases are at least ½" thick. Cut stalks at ground level or hand pull whole stalks.

- **Tips:** The bottom, stem part of the lemongrass plant is the part that you eat. Peel away the outer layer to expose the heart of the stem. It should be white and reedy. Freeze to store.

- **Consider this:** Leave plenty of space around lemongrass to ensure good root growth.

Lettuce

- **Starting:** Start seeds indoors ¼" deep, eight weeks before the last expected frost date.

- **Planting:** Transplant into garden when seedlings are four weeks old. 4 plants per sq. ft.

- **Harvest:** 28 days for baby lettuce, 45 for mature leaves. Can be harvested any time.

- **Tips:** Provide afternoon shade in warm weather to prevent wilting and stress on the plant. A stressed plant is much more susceptible to pests and disease. Plant more lettuce every two to four weeks to keep up a good supply.

- **Consider this:** Aphids love to eat lettuce. Plant chives or garlic between your lettuce to control aphids and act as "barrier plants."

Lunchbox Pepper

- **Starting:** Start seeds indoors ¼" deep, eight to ten weeks before the last expected frost date.

- **Planting:** Transplant into garden when soil reaches 65 degrees F or two weeks after last frost. 1 per sq. ft.

- **Harvest:** 70 days to full maturity. Harvest when pepper is bright orange.

- **Tips:** Humid weather could invite fungal diseases like leaf spot. Make sure your plants have adequate air circulation and aren't sitting in standing water.

- **Consider this:** As lunchbox peppers begin to produce fruit, you may have to provide a stake.

Marjoram

- **Planting:** Perennial in zones 9 and 10. Transplant starter plants into the garden when there is no more threat of frost. 4 plants per sq. ft.

- **Harvest:** 30-45 days to maturity. Harvest sprigs as needed. Trim leaves just after flowers buds appear and before they open. Remove no more than a third of the leaves in a single harvest.

- **Tips:** Trim plants when buds appear and before they flower to ensure continued growth.

- **Consider this:** Marjoram has no serious pest problems but may occasionally be visited by aphids and spider mites. Simply spray them away with a strong stream of water.

Miniature Rose

- **Planting:** Start rose plant in garden after all danger of frost has passed. 1 per sq. ft. Perennial in zones 5-11.

- **Harvest:** Enjoy vibrant blooms throughout the growing season and cut for indoor flower arrangements when desired.

- **Tips:** Prune miniature roses just before new growth starts in late winter or early spring. Prune dead or broken wood to encourage new growth and trim back ⅓" of the plant.

- **Consider this:** Powdery mildew can be a problem so make sure to provide adequate airflow around your rose plant.

Moonflower

- **Planting:** Sow seeds directly in garden ¼" deep when soil reaches 50 degrees F or danger of frost has passed. 1 per sq. ft.

- **Harvest:** Enjoy gorgeous, scented blooms in the evening during the warmer months of the year.

- **Tips:** Install a trellis and lightly twist the vine around it as it grows.

- **Consider this:** Soak seeds overnight before planting to encourage germination.

Morning Glory

- **Planting:** Sow seeds directly into the garden after last frost when soil has warmed to about 65 degrees F. 2 plants per sq. ft.

- **Harvest:** Simply wait until the flowers are spent and begin to dry. Collect the seed pod that forms at the end of the stem. Crack one of these hard, brown pods open. If it has black seeds in it, the pods are ready for harvest. Break seed pods open on a plate lined with a paper towel and let dry for at least one week.

- **Tips:** Provide a trellis, railing, or twine structure to support the trailing morning glory vine to prevent it from taking over the bed.

- **Consider this:** Keep an eye out for wayward morning glory sprouts in your garden as they have a tendency to self-seed.

Mustard Greens

- **Planting:** Start seeds directly in the garden three weeks before the last expected frost date. Sow thickly and thin to 9 per sq. ft.

- **Harvest:** Begin harvesting in about 30 days or when plants are 4" to 6" long.

- **Tips:** Harvest the entire plant before hot weather causes it to bolt.

- **Consider this:** Keep an eye out for any pests munching on the leaves and spray them off with a hose when necessary.

Mustard Seed

- **Planting:** Start seeds directly in the garden three weeks before the last expected frost date. Sow thickly and thin to 2 per sq. ft.

- **Harvest:** Once mustard greens flower and go to seed, they will begin forming seed pods. Wait for these pods to turn brown and harvest as soon as the leaves of the plant begin to turn yellow.

- **Tips:** Place stems in a paper bag and allow pods to burst open. After about two weeks, gently shake the bag and the remaining seeds will fall to the bottom.

Nasturtium

- **Starting:** Start seeds indoors, six to eight weeks before the last expected frost date.

- **Planting:** Transplant seedlings into the garden after last frost. 1 plant per sq. ft.

- **Harvest:** 35-50 days to flower. Collect seeds as flowers dry up and seeds fall to the ground. Store in a cool, dark place.

- **Tips:** Nick one edge of the seed with a metal file before planting. This will help speed germination

- **Consider this:** Nasturtium flowers and seeds are edible and have a slightly peppery taste. Add some to your favorite salads.

Nicotiana

- **Starting:** Start seeds indoors ⅛" deep, six weeks before the last expected frost date.

- **Planting:** Transplant into garden when all danger of frost has passed. 1 per sq. ft.

- **Harvest:** Enjoy this annual plant while the weather stays warm.

- **Tips:** Keep an eye out for aphids and gnats and use natural insect repellent as needed.

- **Consider this:** Plants will likely reseed for next season. Thin as needed when the new seedlings pop up or remove spent flowers right away to avoid reseeding.

Night Phlox

- **Starting:** Start seeds indoors ¼" deep, three to four weeks before the last expected frost date.

- **Planting:** Transplant into garden after danger of frost has passed. 1 per sq. ft.

- **Harvest:** Enjoy this annual plant throughout the spring and summer growing season.

- **Tips:** Pinch off spent blossoms to encourage more flowers.

- **Consider this:** Night phlox is highly fragranced and has a delightful honey and vanilla like aroma. Enjoy its beautiful scent!

Oda pepper

- **Starting:** Start seeds indoors ¼" deep, twelve weeks before the last expected frost date.

- **Planting:** Transplant into garden when soil reaches 65 degrees F or two weeks after last frost. 1 per sq. ft.

- **Harvest:** 70 days to full maturity. Peppers should be a bright purple color at harvest.

- **Tips:** Freeze or refrigerate peppers after harvesting.

- **Consider this:** These plants are short and compact, perfect for growing in containers.

Onion

- **Planting:** Plant onion sets directly 1" deep in the garden as soon as the ground can be worked in the spring. Temperatures should not drop below 20 degrees F. 16 per sq. ft.

- **Harvest:** 90 days to maturity. Ready to harvest when the bulbs are bulging out of the ground and the tops begin to turn yellow and shrivel. Pull them up and leave the tops on to allow the onions to cure. Lay them in a warm, dry place for at least 10 days.

- **Tips:** Clip off the tops and roots of the onions after they have dried and shake off any excess dirt. Be sure not to damage the papery skin as this protects the onions and makes them easier to store.

- **Consider this:** Keep an eye out for weeds as onions are very sensitive and won't grow with competition.

Oregano

- **Planting:** Plant seeds directly into the garden after the threat of frost has passed when soil is about 70 degrees F. Perennial plant. 2 per sq. ft.

- **Harvest:** Harvest right before oregano flowers for optimal flavor. Otherwise, collect leaves as needed throughout the growing season.

- **Tips:** Cut the stems just above the plant's lowest set of leaves for a big harvest in late summer. This encourages new growth for the next cutting.

- **Consider this:** Pick off any browning or spotted foliage to help protect from disease and prevent spread.

Pacino Sunflower

- **Planting:** Sow seeds directly into garden 1" deep when soil reaches 55-60 degrees F or two weeks before the last expected frost date. 4 plants per sq. ft.

- **Harvest:** Seeds are usually ready for harvest 30-45 days after flower blooms. Heads should be finished blooming and starting to brown.

- **Tips:** Hang heads upside down in a garage or basement to dry for a few weeks. Pluck seeds out with a fork or your hands.

- **Consider this:** Protect sunflower heads from birds by covering them with a thin layer of cheesecloth and a rubber band.

Paprika

- **Starting:** Start seeds indoors ¼" deep, twelve weeks before the last expected frost date.

- **Planting:** Transplant into garden when soil reaches 65 degrees F or two weeks after last frost. 1 per sq. ft.

- **Harvest:** 85 days to full maturity. Harvest when completely solid in color.

- **Tips:** Dry paprika peppers in a dehydrator or leave outdoors in the sun on a cookie tray. Turn often and bring indoors if rain is forecast.

- **Consider this:** When peppers are dry and crumbly, simply grind them in a coffee grinder until a coarse powder is formed. Store spice in an airtight spice jar.

Parsley

- **Starting:** Start seeds indoors 1/4" deep, ten to twelve weeks before the last expected frost date.

- **Planting:** Transplant into garden four weeks before last expected frost date. 4 per sq. ft.

- **Harvest:** 75 days to maturity. Harvest any time.

- **Tips:** Parsley seeds take up to 21 days to germinate. Treat with hot water before sowing to encourage growth. Cut off the outer stalks close to the ground using scissors rather than plucking off upper leaves and leaving bare stalks.

- **Consider this:** Biennial in mild climates. Enjoy harvesting throughout the second growing season before planting new seeds the following spring.

Penta

- **Planting:** Plant small transplants directly into the garden after all danger of frost has passed. 1 per sq. ft.

- **Harvest:** The brightly colored cluster blooms will attract all kinds of butterflies and other beneficial pollinators.

- **Tips:** Keep the quick-growing plant in shape with regular pruning.

- **Consider this:** Pentas may be subject to aphid infestation. Control minor issues with a quick spray from a pressurized hose.

Peppermint

- **Planting:** Transplant medium-sized plants into garden after last frost. Leave plants in their containers and bury the containers. This will keep them from taking over your garden. 1 plant per sq. ft. Perennial.

- **Harvest:** Harvest leaves and stems as desired.

- **Tips:** Just before the plant blooms, when the flavour is most intense, cut the whole plant to just above the first or second set of leaves. This will allow new growth.

- **Consider this:** Mint is an invasive herb so bury it in a bottomless pot in the garden with 1-2" showing to prevent takeover.

Petunia

- **Planting:** Place transplants directly into garden after all danger of frost has passed. 1 per sq. ft.

- **Harvest:** Enjoy throughout the summer growing season. Petunias will grow quickly and hang over your raised bed to add a unique trailing element.

- **Tips:** Deadhead regularly to promote blooming.

- **Consider this:** The tobacco budworm is a serious petunia pest. Keep an eye out for any of these harmful critters and remove them by hand or with a natural pest killer.

Pineapple Sage

- **Planting:** Perennial in zones 8-11. Transplant starter plants in spring one to two weeks before last frost. 1 plant per sq. ft.

- **Harvest:** Enjoy harvesting leaves and flowers as needed throughout the growing season.

- **Tips:** Northern zones can dig up pineapple sage in the winter and bring indoors or provide other protection such as mulch to help it survive the cold season.

- **Consider this:** Hummingbirds and butterflies love the vibrant flowers. Enjoy watching beautiful wildlife enjoy your plant.

Poppy

- **Planting:** Sow seeds directly in the garden in early spring about one month before the last expected frost. Scatter seeds and lightly pat into the soil. Thin to 4 per sq. ft. once seedlings begin to sprout.

- **Harvest:** Cut stems for bouquets when blooms are just open.

- **Tips:** Poppies will grow fairly quickly once cut, so harvest frequently.

- **Consider this:** Poppy seeds need fairly cold weather to germinate. If you live in an area with a mild climate, plant poppy seeds in early winter.

Pumpkin

- **Planting:** Pumpkins do best directly sown into the ground when the soil is 70 degrees F or warmer. If you have a short growing season, plant seeds indoors a couple of weeks before the last frost to give them a running start. 1 plant per sq. ft.

- **Harvest:** 95-120 days from seed to fruit. When the plant has died down and skin on pumpkins is firm, cut pumpkins carefully off of the vine using a clean, sharp knife.

- **Tips:** Provide a trellis or position your garden box by a fence so that this vining plant has a sturdy climbing platform.

- **Consider this:** Use mini pumpkins as part of an indoor fall display. They look awesome when grouped with gourds and other fall decor.

Radish

- **Planting:** Plant seeds 1/2" deep directly into the garden four weeks before the last expected frost date. Sow 16 seeds per sq. ft.

- **Harvest:** 21-28 days to maturity. Harvest as soon as possible to prevent bitter flavor.

- **Tips:** Sow radish seeds in any unused area of the garden to utilize the empty space. Plant more seeds as the vegetables mature.

- **Consider this:** Use garden fabric (row covers) to deter cabbage worms and flea beetles that could damage the crop.

Raspberry

- **Planting:** Transplant small plants into garden after last frost. 1 per sq. ft. Perennial in zones 5-9.

- **Harvest:** This dwarf raspberry bush will begin producing fruit in midsummer. Plant will produce even more in subsequent years.

- **Tips:** Remove all dead canes with no growth at ground level in late spring in the second growing season.

- **Consider this:** As with most berries, birds will attempt to steal raspberries, keep them protected with netting, if necessary. Don't let the netting touch the plant as this could interfere with growth.

Red Pepper

- **Starting:** Start seeds indoors ¼" deep, twelve weeks before the last expected frost date.

- **Planting:** Transplant into garden when soil reaches 65 degrees F or two weeks after last frost. 1 per sq. ft.

- **Harvest:** 65-85 days to full maturity. More mature peppers will have better flavor.

- **Tips:** Pinch off early blossoms to encourage larger peppers and a higher yield.

- **Consider this:** Ripe rot can occur when peppers are kept in a warm, humid environment as they ripen. Store harvested peppers in fridge or freezer to prevent this from developing.

Rosemary

- **Planting:** A perennial plant in planting zones 9 or higher. Grow from potted plants once all danger of frost has passed. 1 per sq. ft.

- **Harvest:** Harvest any time once established. Trim sprigs as needed.

- **Tips:** Rosemary is a perennial and will grow more vigorously after its first growing season.

- **Consider this:** Dried rosemary is delicious and is a great way to preserve excess harvest.

Sage

- **Planting:** Perennial in zones 5 to 8. Transplant starter plants in spring one to two weeks before last frost. 1 plant per sq. ft.

- **Harvest:** Harvest leaves as needed once the plant has established roots. Only lightly harvest in the first year to avoid killing the tender plant.

- **Tips:** Prune back plants every year in early spring to promote new growth. Thin plants regularly to encourage air circulation and prevent mildew.

- **Consider this:** Sage may lose flavor and become "woody" after three to five years so it may be a good idea to dig up your old bush in the fall. You will most likely notice new growth in the spring but you may have to plant new starters.

Scallions

- **Starting:** Start seeds indoors ¼" deep, six weeks before the last expected frost date.

- **Planting:** Transplant into garden two weeks before last frost. 16 plants per sq. ft.

- **Harvest:** 60 days to maturity. Scallion should be about the width of a pencil.

- **Tips:** For milder scallions, harvest earlier. Flavor intensifies as they mature.

- **Consider this:** Onion Nematodes are microscopic worms that live in the soil and inject toxins into scallion root systems that cause the tops to turn yellow. Discard the entire affected plant and practice crop rotation.

Scented Geraniums

- **Planting:** Grow scented geraniums from small plants after the last expected frost. 1 per sq. ft.

- **Harvest:** Pluck leaves anytime and rub between your fingers or simply brush against the plant to release the intoxicating scent.

- **Tips:** They are totally edible. Use the leaves or flowers to flavor jams, teas, and baked goods.

- **Consider this:** Scented geraniums include a wide variety of beautiful fragrances including apple, apricot, cinnamon, ginger, lemon, nutmeg, orange, strawberry, rose, peppermint, and chocolate.

Sedum

- **Planting:** Sedum is one of the easiest succulents to grow and all you need is a cutting of the plant. Simply push the cut end of the stalk into the soil and it will develop roots and start producing offshoots. Sedum is a perennial. 2 per sq. ft.

- **Harvest:** Autumn joy sedum is beautiful and puts on a dazzling color show in the fall just as your other plants are winding down. Enjoy its vibrant colors as it stands unrivaled during the cooler season.

- **Tips:** Sedum will dry up in winter, but will return full force once the weather warms.

- **Consider this:** Divide plants in the fall to control spread and keep sedum plants healthy.

Snap Peas

- **Planting:** Sow seeds directly 1" deep into the garden after the danger of frost has passed. 9 per sq. ft.

- **Harvest:** 50-60 days to maturity. Once snap peas start to develop, check each day to enjoy them with that perfect crunch.

- **Tips:** Eat raw straight from the garden and let your kids enjoy hunting through the plants to find ripe peas. Harvest as soon as they are ripe. When peas are left on the plant for too long they can become pithy and lose flavor.

- **Consider this:** Provide some type support such as a twine structure, trellis, or cage.

Snapdragon

- **Starting:** Start seeds indoors eight to ten weeks before the last expected frost date. Lightly pat seeds into the soil. Snapdragon seeds need light to germinate.

- **Planting:** Transplant seedlings a few weeks before the last expected frost. 2 per sq. ft.

- **Harvest:** Use clean scissors or pruning shears to cut the stems as they are too thick to break by hand.

- **Tips:** Regularly deadhead snapdragons to encourage lush blooms.

- **Consider this:** Arrow snapdragons grow up to two feet tall and are excellent for adding height to floral arrangements.

Spearmint

- **Planting:** Transplant medium-sized plants into garden after last frost. Leave plants in their containers and bury the pots. This will keep them from taking over your garden. 1 plant per sq. ft.

- **Harvest:** Harvest leaves and stems as desired.

- **Tips:** Just before the plant blooms, when the flavour is most intense, cut the whole plant to just above the first or second set of leaves. This will allow new growth.

- **Consider this:** Mint is an invasive herb so bury it in a bottomless pot in the garden with 1-2" showing to prevent takeover

Spinach

- **Planting:** Plant seeds directly into the garden as soon as the soil can be worked. Plant a successive crop every two weeks in early spring. 9 per sq. ft.

- **Harvest:** Harvest outer leaves as soon as they are big enough to eat. Leave the inner leaves to allow the plant to keep producing. Spinach leaves can be easily frozen and enjoyed throughout the year or eaten fresh.

- **Tips:** When spinach is about to bolt (go to seed) in late spring, pull the entire plant out to enjoy the last harvest before the leaves become bitter.

- **Consider this:** Spinach is a cool season plant and won't survive through the hot days of summer. Enjoy it in the early spring and plant again in the fall if you live in a climate with a mild winter. Or provide a cold frame for protection.

St. John's Wort

- **Starting:** Start seeds indoors ¼" deep, six to eight weeks before the last expected frost date. Soak seeds overnight before planting to encourage germination.

- **Planting:** Transplant into garden after last frost. Perennial in zones 5-9. 1 plant per sq. ft.

- **Harvest:** Only harvest from St. John's Wort in the second year of growth after the plant flowers. Cut down about ⅓ of the plant and hang the stems to dry.

- **Tips:** St. John's Wort could become leggy so it is important to trim it down at least once each growing season.

- **Consider this:** This plant is deer resistant and isn't susceptible to many bugs or diseases so it is a good choice if you struggle with pests.

Statice

- **Starting:** Start seeds indoors eight weeks before the last expected frost date. Simply scatter them in the growing medium and cover lightly with soil.

- **Planting:** Transplant seedlings into garden after last frost. 1 per sq. ft.

- **Harvest:** Cut stems when flowers are fully open. Tie with rubber band and hang upside down to dry.

- **Tips:** Statice comes in a wide array of colors including rose, white, pink, yellow, peach, and violet shade. Choose the one that suits your interior decor and other dried flowers best.

- **Consider this:** Statice thrives on mild neglect. Be sure not to over water or over-fertilize.

Stevia

- **Planting:** Perennial in planting zone 9 and warmer. Transplant small plants into the garden after all danger of frost has passed. 1 plant per sq. ft.

- **Harvest:** Harvest in midsummer before plants bloom and dry. Or use fresh throughout the growing season.

- **Tips:** Pinch or trim back the plant often to encourage bushiness and prevent premature flowering.

- **Consider this:** Stevia is sensitive to soggy soil so make sure not to overwater.

Stinging Nettle

- **Starting:** Start seeds indoors ¼" deep, four to six weeks before the last expected frost date.

- **Planting:** Transplant into garden after last frost. 1 per sq. ft.

- **Harvest:** Harvest between 80-90 days from seed starting. You'll want to harvest the top few leaves when the plants are still young and tender. Harvest throughout the growing season but always take only the top leaves.

- **Tips:** There's a reason it's called stinging nettle! Protect your hands with thick gloves and wear long sleeves when harvesting this plant.

- **Consider this:** Lay the leaves out to dry on a screen for at least two weeks. Drying will disable the stinging and will allow you to handle the leaves safely.

Stock

- **Starting:** Start seeds indoors 1/8" deep, eight to ten weeks before the last expected frost date.

- **Planting:** Transplant into garden around the time of the last frost. Stock plants need a period of cold for optimal growth. 4 per sq. ft.

- **Harvest:** Stock flowers have an intriguing spicy-sweet fragrance. Gently run your hand through the plant to release the scent.

- **Tips:** Clip stems for cut flower arrangements just as they open or deadhead frequently to promote new growth.

- **Consider this:** Plants will stop blooming and go to seed when temperatures stay above 80 degrees F so enjoy the fragrant flowers in the early spring and summer

Strawflower

- **Planting:** Sprinkle strawflower seeds directly into garden once danger of frost has passed. Don't cover with soil. Once seedlings are three inches tall, thin to 1 per sq. ft.

- **Harvest:** Harvest before the centers of the flowers open so there is enough moisture in the flowers to make them easy to handle. Cut stems 12-14" long and remove the leaves.

- **Tips:** Tie stems together and hang upside for two to three weeks in a dry, dark, well ventilated spot.

- **Consider this:** Harvest regularly to encourage more blooming throughout the growing season.

Swiss Chard

- **Starting:** Start seeds indoors 1/2" deep, six weeks before the last expected frost date.

- **Planting:** Transplant into garden around the last frost. 9 plants per sq. ft.

- **Harvest:** 30 days from seed for baby greens, 50 days to full size.

- **Tips:** Swiss chard is a great summer green as it tolerates heat better than lettuce and kale.

- **Consider this:** Keep an eye out for cercospora leaf spot, a disease that disfigures the leaves with ash-gray spots that have purple edges.

Thai Hot Peppers

- **Starting:** Start seeds indoors ¼" deep, eight to ten weeks before the last expected frost date.

- **Planting:** Transplant into garden when soil reaches 65 degrees F or two weeks after last frost. 1 per sq. ft.

- **Harvest:** 80 days to full maturity. Harvest when peppers are bright red and about 1" long.

- **Tips:** Peppers hate soggy soil. Make sure not to overwater.

- **Consider this:** Wear gloves when harvesting to prevent transfer of oils to your skin. Hot peppers can cause eye damage if you rub your eyes after handling.

Thyme

- **Planting:** Start young plants directly outdoors when soil temperatures reach 70 degrees F or after all danger of frost has passed. 1 per sq. ft. Perennial in zones 5-9.

- **Harvest:** Trim off thyme sprigs as needed once the plant has started to produce new growth. Strip the leaves from the woody stems before using.

- **Tips:** Cut thyme back by ⅓" in the spring after the first growing season. Always cut above points where you can see new growth.

- **Consider this:** Ensure good drainage and air circulation in humid climates to prevent root rot.

Verbena

- **Planting:** Verbena seeds take a long time to germinate so it is best to simply purchase young plants from the nursery. Set out plants after all danger of frost has passed. 1 per sq. ft.

- **Harvest:** Blooms all season until the first frost.

- **Tips:** Cut back verbena plants when they begin to look lanky to extend the growing season.

- **Consider this:** Verbena is subject to various pests. Use a natural pest control method that won't interfere with or harm butterflies.

Watermelon

- **Planting:** Start seeds indoors six to eight weeks before soil warms after last frost. 1 plant per sq. ft.

- **Harvest:** 75 - 80 days to maturity. Cut off of the vine with a clean and sharp knife.

- **Tips:** Vines can grow up to 12 feet. Provide a sturdy trellis to promote air circulation and healthy fruit.

- **Consider this:** Sugar Baby variety of watermelon requires consistent irrigation, drip is best.

Yolo Wonder Bell Peppers

- **Starting:** Start seeds indoors ¼" deep, twelve weeks before the last expected frost date.

- **Planting:** Transplant into garden when soil reaches 65 degrees F or two weeks after last frost. 1 per sq. ft.

- **Harvest:** Collect peppers once they have passed full maturity and are beginning to wrinkle. Slice seeds out of pepper and lay out on a paper plate to dry for at least two weeks.

- **Tips:** Store in an airtight jar or container in a cool, dark place.

- **Consider this:** Pinch off early blossoms on pepper plants to help direct nutrients into producing more fruit.

Zinnias

- **Planting:** Sow seeds directly into the garden, ¼" deep, after the last expected frost date. 9 seeds per sq. ft. Thin to 4 plants per sq. ft when seedlings are three inches tall.

- **Harvest:** 65-70 days from seed to flower.

- **Tips:** Allow your kids to select the varieties and colors and create a living masterpiece. Zinnias make great cut flowers and your kids will love making arrangements for the kitchen table or their bedroom.

- **Consider this:** Zinnias are easy to grow but could be susceptible to powdery mildew if grown too close together. Make sure to thin foliage to allow for air circulation between plants.